Also by Rodney Lacroix

Things Go Wrong For Me
(when life hands you lemons, add vodka)

Perhaps I've Said Too Much
(A Great Big Book of Messing With People)

Romantic As Hell

Tales of woe, Tips of woo

by Rodney Lacroix

Rodney Lacroix has asserted his right under the Copyright, Designs and Patents Act 1988 to be identified as the author of this work.

Any representations of people or products or brand names or trademarks here within are property of the original copyright holders.

This book is a work of non-fiction, sort of, and any resemblance to actual persons, living or dead, is purely on purpose. See how I did that?

Copyright © 2015 Rodney Lacroix – RodneyLacroix.com

All rights reserved under International and Pan-American Copyright Conventions.

Book Illustrations by Noreen Conway.

Cover design by Christina Evans.

Published by RCG Publishing – RCGPublishing.com

Physical Book ISBN-10: 0982772076
Physical Book ISBN-13: 978-0-9827720-7-2

I would like to dedicate this book to my ridiculously beautiful wife, Kerri, who inspires me to outdo myself in the romance department each and every day.
Honey, please stop being so awesome.
This is getting exhausting.

A Note From The Editor

The third book ... *Rodney Lacroix's* third book.

shakes head and closes eyes

When I convinced Rodney to write his first book, I never knew he had so much worthless drivel to share. But he did. He had volumes of it waiting to spill onto the page in the form of run-on sentences and misplaced modifiers.

And boy was it fun to read.

I had a large part in shaping the first and second books, but this one was all Rodney. He came up with the idea and format on his own. Then changed it. And changed it again. It's 100% original in every way.

And you're going to love it.

With stories told in Rodney's unique voice, **Romantic as Hell** shares some great tips and ideas on how to treat your special someone. And unfortunately, it also contains Rodney's trademark gaffs on what *not* to do.

First-time readers of Rodney will love the book for its insights and humor. Long-time fans will love the book because they'll meet a side of Rodney they never knew existed. The human side.

I mean that in a good way.

- Ross Cavins

Introduction

You, my friend, are about to read my third book.

After the success of my first two books, I was a bit stumped on what to approach as the subject matter. Turning to my publisher/editor, I asked him what I should write next, and he simply said:

"Write what you know."

With that advice in mind, I started writing a book about erectile dysfunction. Unfortunately, it ended up as a small pile of sticky-notes with sad-faced penis drawings on them, all stained with my tears.

I then turned to the next thing I know how to do very well: parenting. That project was also canned early because the children would not leave me the hell alone long enough to write a single page. Why can't children open yogurt themselves without repainting the kitchen walls in strawberry-banana? It boggles the mind.

My wife, Kerri, then suggested I write a book on "romance tips."

I couldn't disagree with her on this one, mainly because she wins most arguments anyway. To her point, though, over time I have somehow managed to master the art of wooing. "The Art of Woo" sounds like a contemporary soft-rock band. The Art of Woo would release one single called "Shame Is Forever," and then fade into obscurity. They should have chosen a better name.

This book was originally written as a "How To" type of book. It had projects and crafts that would have made Martha Stewart proud, and maybe even a little fidgety in her panty area. After reading it she would become obsessed with having me, and then I'd hit it, and she would call it "a good thing" and we would laugh and she'd kill a pig with her bare hands so she could make me breakfast sausages.

If you've never read anything of mine before, this is how the entire book is going to go. Fair warning.

After reading **Romantic As Hell** in its original format, I realized the layout and projects—although awesome and boner-inducing—didn't sound like they came from my voice. It was also pointed out that you can find most everything I wrote posted on Pinterest, so my dream of a Martha Stewart amateur porn video went right out the window.

Sometimes I really hate the Internet.

A complete overhaul ensued, and the result is what you now have sitting before you. Each chapter is called an "Act," and is introduced as if I'm presenting it as a theatrical event. This is ironic, because I hate theater unless it's a production of *Sweeney Todd*. What I'm saying is, don't be surprised by the opening format of the chapters and also don't be shocked if I kill off all the main characters by slicing their throats open in a barber's chair.

My overall goal is to make *you* look better in the eyes of your partner, along with a boatload of face-palms and laughs. If you already experienced some of this with the picture of the limp dicks two pages ago, I'd call that a good start.

Enjoy.

Instructions Before Proceeding

MEN: *Please proceed immediately to the next page. Do not follow the instructions for the ladies unless you are confused about your sexuality (or confident in it, whatever).*

LADIES: *Meet me at the very last section of this book for a special message before continuing. Wear something slinky.*

PRELUDE - THE STAGE IS SET

"Prelude" Means "Before the Lewdness"

A small boy wanders out onto the stage in front of a quiet, fidgeting audience. He stops dead center on the platform and looks blankly into a sea of people who are, for the most part, still looking down into their laps because they're playing Candy Crush on their iPhones.

In their defense, it's pretty addicting even though Level 65 is a real bitch.

The boy pauses, nonplussed. He holds up a large poster-board that reads: *The Quest ...*

trumpets blare from the orchestra and the startled boy drops the sign

43 members of the audience crap themselves, and five of them drop their phones. One guy cracks his screen and yells SONOFABITCH I WAS JUST ABOUT TO CLEAR LEVEL 65

Candy Crush, Level 65: *Ruining people's lives since 2012.*

The boy retrieves the sign from the stage floor and holds it aloft again. You finish reading it: *The Quest for the Perfect Gift.*

Face it, we've all been there at one time or another: on the prowl for a special something for that special someone to show her that she's, well, special. I'm not talking *special* special, but *romantically* special. I'm not saying you can't have something *romantically* special with someone who is *special* special, because I'm not a complete a-hole.

Also, I've written *special* so many times now that the word "special" looks really weird to me. Does it look weird to you? I forget where I was going with this. Ah, yes.

The Quest for the Perfect Gift.

trumpets die out in a terrible fart-like sound because that paragraph went on far too long

As the curtain to the stage draws open we find our underdog—you—standing at the entrance of a Hallmark Store, hands jammed deep in pockets, mouth agape. Slowly your head turns from side to side, scanning ... searching. Like the *Terminator*, thrust into an unknown world to hunt down Sarah Conner (the hot Sarah from the first movie, before she got all spindly, muscly, and gross) a heads-up display appears before you.

SEEKING ... SEEKING ... SEEKING

Clerk: Can I help you, sir?

You turn to face the cheerful employee who is only asking because it is required, and her manager is watching. Your display flashes:

Subject: Store Employee ...

Query: Asking to help you ...

Proper responses: "Yes please," "No thank you," "Maybe," "I'm not sure," "What year is it?" and "Kill me now, this is torture."

You: I'm not sure.

Clerk: Well, if you need any help, let me know.

You: Kill me now, this is torture.

The clerk smiles and runs into the back.

Realizing that you just lost the only friend who could possibly help your quest, you return to scanning the store. The smell of Yankee Candles (What is that? Apple? Cinnamon? Death?), Vera Bradley purses, and potpourri overwhelms you. Cautiously you step over the bodies of several men who came in here with their wives hours earlier—each wearing a death-mask stare that says, "Why?"

Ignoring them, but heeding their fate for future visits, you pray that joyous cherubs will appear from the ether, and the aisles will part like the Red Sea, and a quintessential keepsake will illuminate from the rear wall of the store, as if it were screaming, "HERE I AM, EXACTLY THE GIFT YOU NEED!"

But nothing happens.

No inspiration comes to you, and the only person you see resembling a cherub is the nice lady behind the counter wrapping fudge. You are alone in a sea of paisley wallets, weird-looking figurines with large eyeballs and heads that defy biological accuracies, and—of course—the whole counter of Alex and Ani bracelets[1].

That Eureka feeling you so desire eludes you.

Resigned to your fate, you slowly turn left and begin trudging through the aisles. Each step is deliberate and includes calculations that would make Albert Einstein quiver with fear.

1. Lift foot up.

2. Move leg forward.

3. Turn head left.

4. Scan up.

5. Scan down.

6. Place foot down.

7. Turn head right.

8. Scan up.

9. Scan down.

---

[1] "Alex and Ani" is a $100 million dollar company that makes bracelets, mostly from recycled materials, in case you needed another reason to question your life's decisions as you eat cold spaghetti rings from a can.

Do you see an acceptable item? If *yes*, acquire and proceed to checkout. If *no*, repeat steps 1-9 using other leg.

Time stands still as you wander through aisles of beaded picture frames, painted wine glasses, and fur-covered hand puppets. After spending a few minutes making a puppet talk with a terrible Italian accent that deteriorates into a bad Dracula impression, you continue with your search because you don't want to die in this store like those other poor bastards.

By the time the manager yells, "STORE CLOSING," you realize you have been wandering around for three hours and have lost almost two pounds. Your FitBit is really proud of you, but you still haven't ... wait ...

You look down. You're holding a card in your hand. You barely remember looking at them, but at some point you must have stood in front of the giant wall of cards deciding between funny or smooshy or "For Her" or "From Him" or "Love" or "Like" or "Meh, You're Okay" or the ones that open and OHMYGOD WHY IS THIS ONE SINGING?!

Cover: *To the one I love*

Inside: *Blah blah blah. I looked through 400 cards. This was better than nothing. Blah blah blah.*

That's not what it says, but that's what it *should* say because finding the perfect card is a day trip in and of itself. If you get a card that is 60% of what you would normally say, in a voice you'd normally say it in, that's the winner.

"To my love, our love is like a summer ..." NOPE.

"You are my everything. You are the wind ben-." AYFKM[1] *who talks like that? No.*

"I love you. Thanks for not leaving me for someone better who has abs and doesn't pressure you to do butt stuff."

Awesome. Card requirement? DONE.

But the store is closing, so in desperation, you grab one of those stupid Troll dolls because it's right there at the checkout counter, and it's kind of cute, right?

No, it's terrible, but you're out of time. Maybe you'll throw in a homemade "free backrub coupon" to even it all out. Stop talking now because you're making it worse. You really are terrible at this.

It's okay. Because I was once like you.

That's why I wanted to write this book. With a little perseverance and a lot of trial and error (and some errors that led to trials, but my lawyer will not allow me to discuss those), I have done my best to fix my pathetic ways.

And so, with some innovative ideas and tragic stories in hand, and a word processor at my fingertips, this book began to take shape. If dredging step-by-step through a 300-page book that lists over 1000 supposedly romantic ideas sounds like hell, you've come to the right place.

Take my hand. Walk with me.

I'm about to spin some tales of romantic woe and several tips of romantic woo. Take what you can from these stories and run with them. That is, unless

---

[1] Acronym for "Are You F**king Kidding Me" in case you didn't know that because you're either really old or really young. If you're really young, please return this book to your mom or dad ASAP[2].

[2] Acronym for "As Soon As Possible." Okay, this is starting to get silly.

you're like me and hate doing any type of cardio.

What I'm saying is, don't fall into the same traps and mistakes I've made in the past. What traps and mistakes? Trust me, you'll know them when you read them.

> **Worst Case:** You laugh.
>
> **Better Case:** You laugh AND get some tips that strengthen your position in the dating community or in your own relationship.
>
> **Best Possible Case Ever:** You laugh AND get some good tips AND make your significant other's friends think you're amazing, thus increasing the odds of a threesome.

Always, always, aim for the best possible case ever. I cannot emphasize this enough.

Um, by the way, you do realize you forgot to get her something from the kids, right?

Go on.

I'll be here when you get back.

ACT 1 - THE DAWN OF WOO

"Evolution" Is Just an Anagram for "I Love U Ton"

As the curtain draws open for the first act, we see the stage set up as a barren wasteland. The backdrop reflects a burning sun and the arid, dry air of a scorching day. Obviously, they are reusing the scenery from *The Lion King* musical the third grade put on last month. *Oh my God, when the kid playing Rafiki forgot his line and threw the baby Simba off the cliff in frustration, I thought I was going to die.*

Stage right, a small gelatinous object being dragged by fish-wire emerges from behind a sign that says "Primordial Ooze."

The glop of pink goo disappears behind a cardboard tumbleweed, and a small child in an Ewok suit emerges from the other side. He crawls on all fours and vanishes behind a bigger cardboard tumbleweed where a larger child dressed in a gorilla costume, walking upright, appears.

This makes me think of the time my son dressed up for Halloween as a banana. I laugh out loud and accidentally yell, "BANANA."

Luckily, I'm just one of four people left in the audience, so the only angry glance I get is from the gorilla kid. He glares at me, makes a jerk-off motion in my direction, and disappears behind a giant cactus. A man emerges from the other side wearing a loincloth with a fake mustache taped to his forehead.

AH. I get it. What we're seeing is the evolution of man, if the evolution of man involved really shitty costume choices. It's at this point I sense the production values of this play are non-existent, and I'm glad I didn't pay any money to see this crap.

The Neanderthal man points to stage left, where a female Neanderthal enters from behind a black curtain. He tilts his head and looks confused for a moment. Then he glances down at his crotch with surprise and wonderment.

Caveman boner.

The laws of attraction take over, and this early descendant of man feels drawn toward his female counterpart. As he nears her, she looks shyly away and shuffles her super-hairy feet together.

Ah, I think to myself. *This must take place in Europe.*

Slowly and warily, the caveman approaches the cave-chick. It is clear he's unsure what to do. How does he show this obviously Italian woman how he's feeling? He can't send her a wink because Match.com is still decades away from being invented, so what can he do?

Thinking fast, he reaches down, grabs a giant wooden stick, and bashes her over the skull. She collapses unconscious to the stage.

Thus, the very first roofie is invented.[1]

He bends over, picks her up, and takes her to his place, where the next scene opens.

His bachelor pad is pretty swag for 65,000 BC, with some sweet cave drawings and one of those rock-beds that folds out from the wall. He places her head on the softest piece of granite he can find, and begins preparations as he waits for her to wake up. Of course, he sneaks a couple of peeks at her undercarriage while she's out because even early man mostly thought with his cave-dick.

She wakes soon after, only to find herself covered in a blanket of pine needles, a dead sloth, and what appear to be feces. Thus, the earliest

---

[1] This might not be 100% historically accurate.

Valentine's Day is born, and the caveman's trinkets of flowers, teddy bears, and chocolates become the romantic standby gifts for thousands of years to come. Luckily for us, chocolate replaced the traditional "smearing of feces" around 1893 when Milton Hershey decided it was getting kind of gross.[1]

The cavewoman looks up at the unibrowed man and smiles. Her heart beats harder inside her gross, hairy chest. No one has ever done something like this for her before, primarily because she lives alone with her mom and doesn't get out much.

She swoons at his romantic gestures. By "swoons" I mean "grunts four times and picks out some of his head lice."

Kudos to the caveman for his on-the-fly-thinking. Sadly, flowers, teddy bears, and chocolates are also some of the most overused and clichéd gifts on the planet, but at least now you know how it all began.

So, ladies, when your man arrives at your doorstep with a stupid bear and a 26,000-calorie box of caramels, don't blame him. It's genetic.

---

[1] Thank you, Milton. Thank you.

I. In the Name of the Father, the Son, and Holy Crap That Is a Terrible Idea

"It's not your fault." — **Sean, Good Will Hunting**

"Don't blame me, I was born awesome." — **Me, just now**

"Um. Thanks?"

My wife said this to me after tearing the wrapping paper off her birthday gift. No eye contact was made. She just stared at the sparkling new Black & Decker coffee maker and muttered, "Thanks?" as if it were a question.

Aw, crap.

That certainly wasn't the reaction I was shooting for. Her response was more the confused look of a Catholic coming to the realization that prostate exams are, actually, quite enjoyable.

Man, if I had a nickel ...

I didn't understand. She needed a coffee maker and liked coffee, so it seemed like a no-brainer to me. I bought it on sale and realized there was a setting where you could program it to make your java *before you even woke up.*

Seriously? Did I transport into the future because that was some ridiculously powerful technology sitting at her fingertips.

Long gone would be the days of her having to make her own coffee in the morning, because this machine—obviously a precursor to the *Star Wars* droids—would have already done it for her. It was a miracle, really. A beautiful, birthday miracle that made Breakfast Blend while she slept.

She did not think it a miracle.

I was confused. Not nearly as confused as when I was deciding to confess my feelings about the prostate exam to the priest that always winks at me, but I was perplexed nonetheless.

Even the accompanying giant coffee mug that looked just like the ones from *Friends* didn't garner the "OH I LOVE IT" reaction I was expecting. The mug could have literally held thirteen gallons of coffee. I've pooped three times just thinking about it.

I didn't get it. What did I do wrong? My dad used to get my mom stuff like this all the ti—

eyes go wide

I began thinking back on every gift my mother received from my father:

start television wavy flashback scene here

- *Vacuum cleaners.*
- *Blenders.*
- *Flannel nightgowns fourteen times her actual width and twice her height.*
- *A naughty nightie half her size and someone please kill me right now.*
- *Cleaning supplies.*

Yes. Cleaning supplies.

My mom once received a car-wash bucket with soap and sponges and a squeegee. Admittedly, the squeegee was really, cool but my mom failed to see the awesomeness of it on their 20th anniversary. I can tell you, though, that I used it myself to clean a beer spill off the hood of my car, and it worked fabulously. Plus, "squeegee" is fun to say out loud.

Squeegee squeegee squeegee.

You know I'm not wrong about this, people.

I then flashed back to all thoughtful gifts I had given to women over the years:

- *A memory-foam pillow.*
- *A jar of cashews.*
- *A $25 Gift Card with an extra $20 in Kohl's Cash.*
- *Homemade "Love Coupon" booklets, in a pathetic attempt to get laid but make it look like a present.*
- *That stupid goddamn coffee maker.*

As I sorted through my memory I realized a horrifying truth: My father had genetically passed his God-awful gift-giving genes down to me, his one and only son.

"NOOOOOOOOOOOOOOOOOOOOOOOOOOOOOO!"

I snatched the coffee maker from the countertop, jumped into my car, and fled. I had to right this wrong.

I didn't look back. I didn't say a word.

Then "Runaway" by *Bon Jovi* came on the radio, so I sang that at the top of my lungs. I frigging LOVE that song. You can't *not* sing it. The only way it could be better is if it had "squeegee" in the lyrics.

I dashed into the department store where I bought that damn coffee maker, ran up to the counter, and exchanged it for something else. I asked if the clerk could put the new item in a box for me, and then realized she didn't understand English. After five minutes of yelling

"Box. BOX. BAWWWWXXXX" over and over again in decreasing speeds while making cube shapes with my hands, she figured it out, handed me my new gift, and I was on my way. As an aside, saying "box" really slowly isn't nearly as fun as you'd think.

I returned to the scene of the birthday coffee crime a scant ten minutes later.

Voiceover guy: *NCIS: Maxwell House,*" new on CBS Thursday.

There's a reason I don't write television shows.

"Where the Hell did you go?" she asked.

"Haglebop!" I blurted out, before collapsing in a heap on the floor because I'd been rushing around for a while, and I stress easily.

She took the box and opened it.

Lying in a puddle of my own drool, heart still racing, I glanced up in time to see that same, prostate-exam look on her face as she held out the giant flannel nightgown in front of her.

"Gee. Thanks. It's, like, fourteen sizes too big, though."

I knew I should have gone with the squeegee.

Damn you, Dad. Damn you and your shitty gift DNA.

It was at that moment I felt in my heart that I needed to change. No longer would I, Rodney Lacroix, be the bearer of gifts that prompted the inevitable questions:

> "Do you still have the receipt?" and "Why are you still on the floor? Are you okay?"

The process would take time. It would take dedication. It would require shedding years of learned behavior and rebuilding myself as the greatest romantic gift-giver known to man!

The process also sounded exhausting. It would require many naps.

I wonder if that chick still has the memory-foam pillow I gave her ...

II. Of Genetic Implants, Lingerie, Teddy Bears, and Chocolates

"It's true! I read that somewhere ... I wrote it down and then I read it! I believe everything I read." — **Bob Saget**

We can make excuses all day for why we show little emotion towards, or give really crappy things to, the people we care about. Do we do this instinctively, a function ingrained in us through thousands and thousands of years of evolution?

Why the hell did early man think bonking a woman on the head would endear her to him? Did cavemen invent BDSM? Can we blame our parents for teaching us the wrong way to approach and sustain relationships? Does this thing look infected to you?

Sorry. I got carried away on the questioning.

Maybe there's a bit of truth to all of those things. Maybe there isn't. I'm just here to throw out all the possibilities because I like giving my editors things to do. They get paid by the word, so I'm really shooting myself in the foot at this point.

A lot of environmental factors influence how we form ideas of what is—and is not—romantic. Most of this comes from advertising and believing what we hear and see. If this hypothesis is true, you now believe that Hershey chocolates were invented to replace feces-smearing during a holiday about love, and that cavemen invented Rohypnol.

Also, you're an idiot.

Think, for just a moment, about what you would give (or get) as a *typical* "romantic" gift. The average woman here will say one or more of the following:
- Jewelry.
- Flowers.
- A box of chocolates.
- Lingerie.
- A teddy bear.

Subsequently, there are five staples to every man's notion of what constitutes a romantic gift:
- Jewelry.
- Flowers.
- A box of chocolates.
- Lingerie.
- A teddy bear.

Coincidence? Probably.

Men are a simple folk. We like stuff handed to us so we don't have to think about it too much. Thinking hurts, unless it's about which flavor of buffalo wings to order.

We also will never directly ask a woman what she wants. Doing that is a relationship death-wish, because if you don't already know what she wants, you haven't been paying attention and don't care about her.

This is why men drink.

Plus, we don't think we *need* to ask women. You see, much like how the pack mentality has been ingrained into your puggle's[1] DNA (a result of thousands of years of evolution from wolves), these gift ideas are cemented into the flaccid brains of the average man. This single paragraph has taken me 15 minutes to write because I went off on a daydream of a pack of puggles

---

[1] A puggle is a cross between a pug and a beagle. This was a much more successful cross-breed than the ill-conceived pugdane experiment, which ended up with a lot of really sore female pugs.

running through the forest, attacking a deer and trying to kill it by gnawing at its ankles. Oh my God they're so cute.

Like I said: *the flaccid brains of men*.

Fortunes have been made by smarter people who have identified this weakness and subsequently started their own companies to take full advantage of it. The heart-shaped chocolates box, for instance, was invented by *Nirvana* front-man Kurt Cobain. The now-famous teddy bear was invented by Theodore Roosevelt during his siege on Troy, when his army jumped out of a giant replica of Teddy Ruxpin and successfully conquered Japan.

This is not a history book, people.

Be honest, the only reason men give lingerie to women is because we want to tear it off them. Men, women are well aware that this is your ulterior motive. If lingerie was comfortable, our ladies would wear naughty maid outfits every night. Instead, they slip on oversized purple sweatshirts with pictures of owls on them that say "WHO wants some a dis?"

And women get men ties and shirts because, well, they want their men to be successful. More success means more money. More money means they can buy more comfy owl shirts to sleep in.

It's a vicious cycle.

The closest a woman gets to giving lingerie to a guy is when she gives him underwear with a "penis holder" feature attached (elephant trunk / Pinocchio nose / thimble).

Women get men penis-receptacle underwear because (a) they want to see if you can fill the thing out, and (b) they are going to think it's hysterical when you try.

Worst case, they get a very sad elephant and fifteen minutes of cry-laughing, so it's a win-win for them.

Sometimes, when I type, the repressed memories come back. That was one of those times. Now I'm sad, and so is my tiny Dumbo.

Where was I? Oh, yes. YOU.

Your task, though, as you prepare to give your lover a gift, is to eschew the mundane and go for the extraordinary. Flowers are the exception to this, because flowers are pretty.

Chocolates, however, make you obese and diabetic. No one wants diabetes, and there is not a single man on the planet who wants to answer the "Do these pants make my ass look huge" question honestly, so chocolates should be automatically disqualified from any gift consideration.

Teddy bears, though, *seem* like a cute gift. That is, until you factor in that no one wants to receive one. Statistics show that the number-one ingredient to the "break-up bonfire" she will hold in your honor after you split is a stuffed bear.[1]

So before you pick up the phone and call that company that makes $150 custom stuffed animals that will someday be sold at your yard sale for $3, I've made this flowchart to help you decide if you should get her one:

---

[1] I make up a lot of statistics in this book. This happens to be one of them.

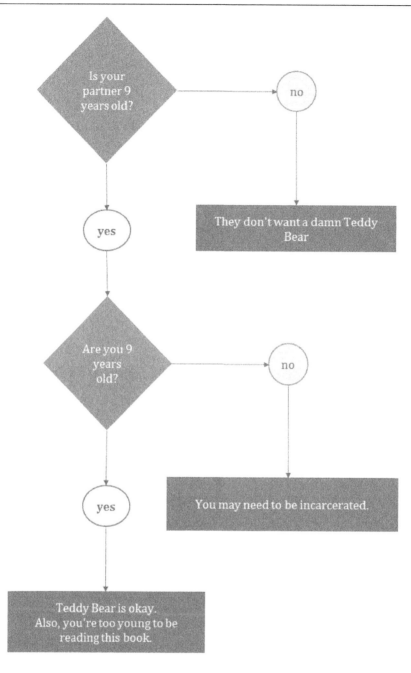

Feel free to reference this flowchart every time you think of getting her that little stuffed animal, and then *don't do it.*

Remember what happened at Troy.

Act 1 Progress Checklist

These handy-dandy checklists will appear at the end of each section so you can track your progress. They also serve as a reminder of the lessons learned while simultaneously making this book appear more substantial.

	Yes	No
Household appliances make women swoon.	☐	☒
Chocolates are not a gift, but instead, a precursor to a lifetime of insulin injections.	☑	☐
Teddy bears are assholes.	☑	☐

ACT 2 - BASIC STRAINING

I. Well, That Was Embarrassing

The stage set changes to the bedroom of a teenage boy.

The wallpaper has a metallic sheen to it, reflecting dark green carpeting. A large waterbed sits against a wall, and tacked to the wall above the bed are two posters: The Dallas Cowboy Cheerleaders and Christie Brinkley. Both posters look worn and crinkly. We will not stop to consider why right now because the answer is probably disturbing. A dresser with a large mirror sits against the opposite wall, adorned with a blue Tiffany lamp.

This looks to be one of the worst-designed rooms of all time and should be on a television home-design show that has the words "Disasters" or "Rescue" in the title.

The bedroom door swings open, and a young man in a denim jacket enters. He stands in the doorway and grabs the chin-up bar above his head. We watch, silently, as he struggles to pull himself up approximately two inches before dropping to the floor in a puddle of sweat. There is a sign on the outer side of the door that reads, *"Rodney's Room"*

Ah. That explains everything.

The boy stands upright, brushes himself off, and heads over to the dresser. He pretends to smash the Tiffany lamp with his fist because he hates that stupid thing so much and wants it to explode into a quadbillion pieces. Yes that's a made-up number, but it cannot be stressed enough how much he wants that thing to disintegrate. You can't really tell this from sitting in the audience because there's no dialogue yet, but trust me, he's thinking it.

He leans into the mirror, licks a finger, and flattens his eyebrows. He smiles at himself, checking to see if there's any trace of leftover Hot Pocket visible between his teeth. He smiles and nods to his reflection.

"Hey," he says to himself.

"Heyyy," again, but this time smoother.

"Heyyyyyyy." Now he's Fonzie. What the hell is going on?!

He turns sideways, then looks over his shoulder at his reflection.

"Hey. How are you?" he asks, giving himself the once-over.

The boy is obviously practicing someth—

He closes his eyes and wraps his arms around an invisible person in front of him. The scene is getting weird and gross. I feel uncomfortable just watching this. What the sweet hell is this kid doing? OHMYGOD NOW HE'S OPENING HIS MOUTH AND DOING A MAKE-OUT FACE.

He turns around, his back to the mirror, and wraps his arms around himself. He glances over his shoulder to see what it's going to look like when he's kissing whoever, and her hands are caressing his back. The boy has some serious issues.

"Hey Rod, I wa—" A woman stops dead in the doorway.

"Mooommmmmmmmmmmmmm!"

"I don't even want to know," she says.

Neither do we, lady. Neither do we.

He shuts the door in her face. His practice abruptly canceled, he turns to face the mirror fully again, checks himself out one more time, and then smiles at the posters over his bed.

"Wish me luck," he says to Christie's wrinkled, stained poster—wait, stained?!

"Date night," he says as he wiggles his left eyebrow.

The boy takes one last look in the mirror and exits the room.

The lights dim, and everyone in the audience gets up to exit as well. They're all going to wash up.

Seriously, that was disturbing to watch.

II. The "Lookie For The Nookie" Tip

"She's got the looks that kill" — **Motley Crue**

"She's got Bette Davis eyes" — **Kim Carnes**

"If Bette Davis and Motley Crue had a baby, I bet it would have laser vision." — **anonymous**

When you embark upon your romantic voyage and begin implementing some of your ideas, you need to start off slowly. That's why we're going to push you off with some basics so you don't strain yourself (the title for this act suddenly reveals itself in glorious splendor).

It's like the old saying goes:

"Before you learn to walk, you have to learn to crawl. Before you learn to crawl, you have to figure out how to roll over because if you don't roll over, your pee goes straight up in the air. No one will find you attractive if you pee straight up in the air because chances are it's getting all over you."

I'm terrible at remembering quotes, although that not-peeing-in-the-air thing seems like sound advice.

Statistics show that 70% of men and women regard the eyes as the feature they notice first in someone of the opposite sex.[1] This statistic drops to 10% in men if the woman they're looking at has big boobs.[2]

Since the eyes are so important, it makes sense to figure out how to use them properly. You already know how to see, unless you're blind and got this book on audiotape (now I feel bad for even mentioning it). For the rest of you,

---

[1] Taken from medicaldaily.com— holy shit I just footnoted an actual fact. *plays lottery*
[2] Also valid if the woman has small boobs but is wearing a padded bra and/or has stiff nips.

though, working on *how* you look at someone is just as important as *if* you do. Especially if you have a lazy or wonky eye. If the latter is the case, this may still be a tough section for you, but do your best.

Right now I can hear you all saying, *"I can't believe I paid for something that tells me to look at someone,"* but bear with me because we're starting out with the easy stuff and working our way up. Also, by the time you've gotten to this point in the book, I've already received a royalty. To gyp[1] me out of any money, you would have had to return it around Page 3 (pursuant to Amazon's ever-changing rules, of course). Keep this tip in mind for the next "50 Shades" book you get.

Back to *The Look*. One of the very first things that can endear someone to you is how you react to them when they walk into the room. This can be

---

[1] I mean no offense to gypsies when I use this term. That is, unless it causes a national outrage which turns into blanket media exposure that catapults me to Best Seller status. Then, sure, be offended and take your anger to a major news outlet. Thank you in advance.

during your initial meeting, before you get intimate, when you walk into the bathroom and they're brushing their teeth, or when you initially meet them in a bathroom and get intimate while they're brushing their teeth.

I'm not here to judge you. Also, you should boil your toothbrushes and disinfect the bathroom sink at some point. You people have no shame. It's disgusting, really.

"The look" is very simple to execute, and even simpler if you don't have to fake it.

1. Look at the person (In the eyes, people. Eyes).
2. Smirk/smile.
3. Let out a short breath (optional, although technically you should be breathing anyway).

Side note: One of my female editors told me to add "(4) Don't look away" as an another step. I did some internet searching, and sure enough, a prolonged gaze is listed as a thing people find alluring.

I didn't put it in because gaping at someone can start to get eerie if it's sustained for longer than ten seconds. It can also be considered the start of a staring contest. If you or your partner is a sore loser, this won't end well, and you'll probably get dry-eye.

The same editor also called a *held stare* her "kryptonite," but the point is to make someone feel sexy and not kill Superman, so I don't get it.

Nevertheless, it doesn't take a lot to make someone feel like she's *the one*. The simple act of actually making eye contact and smiling has been proven to increase romantic response in the recipients by releasing endorphins and chrysanthemums and small neurotoxins. I didn't look that up anywhere, but it sounds good.

However, just so we're clear, here are some "Dos" and "Don'ts" on how to achieve *The Look*.

For the Guys

Guys, to get the right look you have to be subtle and try not to look like a douche. This may be tough in certain areas of the country where guys may truly be douches (New Jersey guys with white sunglasses, for example) or if you find that looking at a woman like that yields results (i.e., strip joints during the Sunday day shift).

Here are the right and wrong ways to look at a woman, and what each implies:

On the *Yes* side, the head-tilt says, "I'm vulnerable to your charms." The smirk says "You are pleasing" or "I have a small piece of apple peel stuck in my molar."

On the *No* side, I realize I look like I just ate bad cheese, but I was going for the "Heyyy ... you look bootaful! DAMN" kind of face.

There's a reason I'm not a model.

Long story short, try the *Yes* side.

For the Ladies

Girls, I can tell you from a man's standpoint that you could literally stare at him cross-eyed with cataracts, and it wouldn't matter. If you look in our general direction, we think you're interested. If you look in a different direction, we think you're interested. There is no way you win this battle unless the guy is visually impaired, and you have a clear and quick exit.

However, if you ARE interested in the guy, I can tell you 100% that the "seductively biting the lip" thing will work for us EVERY. SINGLE. TIME. Every time. There are almost zero exceptions to this except for below:

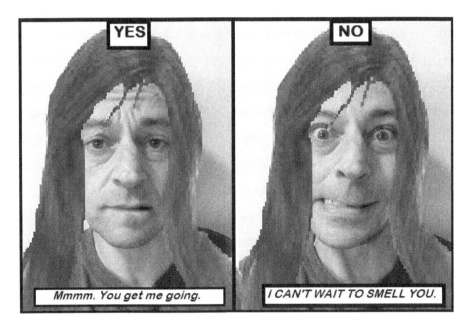

Bite the bottom lip. THE BOTTOM LIP.

I think why is self-explanatory.

Also, please note that I had to copy the hair from a picture I found on the Internet because I could not find my mullet wig, and trust me, I looked everywhere. I'm so sad.

Regardless, you looking at a man while biting your bottom lip will render him helpless. It's like happiness to The Hulk, lobbyists to congressmen, or bad analogies to my writing.

The point is: Men are powerless against the look and bitten-lip technique.

Try it. Take a look at him or her. A good look. And don't forget the smile. The smile on the LEFT.

There. Better.

III. Digitally Remastered

You have now hopefully mastered *The Look* and are laying to waste the hearts of members of the opposite sex everywhere. I'm not talking about wasting hearts in the Jeffrey Dahmer sense, because he ate those people. I guess in a roundabout way, your goal is roughly the same, and I think I'll stop talking now.

The one thing I didn't mention, though, was that *looking* at a person is completely different than *noticing* them.

Whoa. That was deep.

That's what she said.

Never. She's never said that. Not to me, anyway.

runs away to compose self

Do you notice things about your partner's features that no one else does? I mean, like no one else notices unless they pay her $20 for three minutes in the Champagne Room? Just because you look at her all the time doesn't mean you take it all in.

That's what sh—

You know. I'm not even gonna bother on that one.

I once dated a woman for a year, and one night, I reached over and started rubbing her cheekbone with my thumb.

Her: What the hell are you doing?

Me: You have a huge smudge of mascara or something right here.

Her: Stop rubbing it.

Me: UGH. WHY WON'T THIS COME OFF?!

Her: You asshole. Those are freckles.

Me: Oh.

I put my hand down. Out of my peripheral vision I could see her glaring at me, and I asked the inevitable stupid question:

Me: Have you always had those?

Turns out she had. Since, like, birth. But I never noticed them during twelve whole months of dating. Freckles apparently don't appear in giant clusters unless you have skin cancer, she told me. She also called me more names. It was a fun evening.

But that wasn't the worst oversight I've ever had.

The year was 1985 ...

I was sitting at the "cool lunch table" as us cool people coolly did at lunch. I was minding my own cool business, eating my cool sandwich and being cool in the general sense, when I looked across the room and saw a cute girl looking back at me. She gave me *The Look,* and pulled it off with aplomb. I can use that fancy word here because I had just passed a vocab test in English class the period before.

I turned and looked behind me to see who she was really looking at, because even if you're cool, that doesn't mean people find you attractive. Behind me was a wall, which also indicates that "being cool" does not necessarily mean "you're a very smart person aware of your immediate surroundings."

I turned to my friend Greg.

Me: Hey. That chick is checking me out.

Greg: That's Julia. Dude. You don't know? She wants to go out with you.

Me: How do you know?

Greg: She told me.

This is why friends suck. Why Greg failed to inform me that this girl wanted to go out with me is something I question to this very day. Although, there was no "Bro Code" back in the 80s, so I forgive him this transgression, especially since "bro" wasn't a word back then.

I approached Julia after lunch and asked her out.

We went on a few dates, and then a few more. Before I knew it, Rodney and Julia were a boyfriend/girlfriend couple who had been seeing each other for months.

And that's when Greg asked me the question at lunch one day.

Greg: So, what's the deal with her finger?

Um. What?

Me: What do you mean?

Greg: Her finger. What's the story with her finger?

Oh. Thank you for asking me the exact same question again in the exact same way. It's much clearer to me now, jackass.

Me: I HAVE NO IDEA WHAT YOU'RE TALKING ABOUT.

Greg: Dude. She doesn't have a pinky.

This is where, if you're watching a movie and some bombshell has been dropped on a character, or he has some startling realization, the camera does that weird focus thing that makes his face bigger while shrinking the background.

Upon hearing this news, my head exploded and the school turned into a tiny Lego set.

Me: SHUT. UP.

Greg: Are you seriously telling me, right now, that you didn't know?

I didn't know. I had no idea. My friends had no idea that I had no idea. I had no idea that my friends had no idea that I had no idea. This paragraph is rambling, but I think you get the ... never mind.

She had no pinky? Seriously? We had been going out for months. MONTHS.

It is quickly occurring to me that I am the biggest asshole in the history of ever. How do you, at any point during a 4-month relationship, not notice that your girlfriend is missing an entire finger?

This should tell you, ladies, how much more attention men pay to other things, such as your boobs and ass. I'm sure if she'd been missing a butt cheek, I would have noticed immediately.

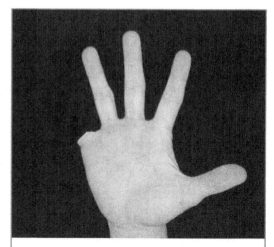

HOW DO I NOT NOTICE THIS?!

Then I thought, *Maybe my friends are just messing with me*. There's no way I'd miss her having only nine fingers. I mean, she'd given me handjobs, and I would have felt that, right? Right?

> **Me:** Hey. That feels weird. Something's not quite ... wait, are you missing a finger?

Julia and I were scheduled to go out that Friday night. I tried to tell myself I wouldn't stare, that it was still the same girl I had been attracted to for months, but in my heart I knew I'd have to at least take a peek just to make sure my buddies weren't dicking me around.

As drove to the movie, I quickly glanced down at Julia's hand.

FIVE FINGERS.

Ha! Suck it, guys. She has all her fin—

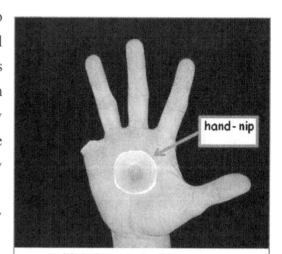

Had her hand looked like this, I would have noticed the finger sooner

Wait. She has two hands. Thank goodness I remembered that from biology class. Hooray for the New Hampshire school system! We good learners!

Pretending to look both ways at a stop sign, I subtly glanced at her other hand resting by her side. There, in all its glory, was a hand sporting only four fingers. The pinky was nowhere to be found.

She glanced toward me, and my gaze returned to looking out her window. She smiled, and gave me a kiss on the cheek. I smiled back, but honestly, I felt a bit heavy in my heart. I really liked her, but in all the times I'd *looked* at her, I'd never once noticed this about her. When all is said and done, how do you not feel guilty about that?

I never gathered up the courage to ask her what happened.

Did I not notice because it didn't matter to me, or did I not see it because I was concentrating on other things that were more conducive to my teenage libido? I guess I'll never know.

So you should master *The Look*, but also take time to *notice* your significant other, too. The small things, the big things, the missing things, and hell, even the extra things (for those of you reading this in India who have 17 toes and stuff).

Take it all in.

I just wish Greg had been messing with me. I would have liked to have seen him on Monday and given him the finger.

I apologize for the terrible pun.

I'm sorry I put it in there.

That's what she said.

IV. The "Chivalry Delivery" Tip

I was going to put a definition here of "chivalry" until I discovered it actually means "horsemanship," and I really didn't want to start this story off by insulting your woman. Feel free to insert any and all "ride a cowboy," "she sure likes carrots," or "ridden hard, put away wet" jokes here.

That reminds me: Jim McMannis, if you're reading this, please come get your mom's spurs because she left them at my house on Friday. Also take her saddle with you, and FYI, I may or may not be your father.

When I think of chivalry, I think of Renaissance Festivals where medieval knights kill each other on a field while a busty maiden with her boobs spilling out tries to sell me a jester's hat for $39.99.

I own 27 jester hats.

To close out this section, I'm going to give you some rough pointers on how to be chivalrous. If you don't have any horses, knights, or busty maids selling overpriced knockoffs handy, this may be difficult for you, but try your best.

We've all heard the phrase, "Chivalry is dead," but right here is where we change it to "Chivalry isn't dead, it's been revived by a strange virus and is now zombified and alive and well in our relationship!"

Please note that none of my sayings are set in stone so feel free to change that to something that fits your situation, just in case you're not a fan of zombies. Loser.

Here's the scoop, men: women love when you do the stupid little things for them that make them feel like they have your entire focus. Acts of chivalry go into this category, while wearing fake "X-Ray Glasses" does not.

As an added benefit, being chivalrous also gives you the edge over other guys—mainly when your woman's friend looks at her own man and says, "Now why don't YOU do stuff like that for me?" Then the guy looks at you and telepathically calls you an asshole.

Remember: making your girl feel good while making other men look bad is the KEY to romance.

I'm adding simple acts of chivalry here because these are things you can do every single day to let her know she has all of your attention.

Open the car door for her.

Cliché, I know. But opening the door for her when she gets into the car is a stupid simple thing that means something special to a woman. Now, when you go to the mall, you don't have to park the car, and like a valet, run over to her door while she waits.

If your woman actually expects you to open the door for her to get *out*, then you are no longer her man. At this point, you have become her bitch. Don't be her bitch.

Close the car door for her.

This seems like an obvious progression after #1, but first be sure that all of her extremities are inside the car. That's important. Learn from my mistakes.

Now that I'm thinking about it, I wonder if that's what happened to Julia's pinky finger.

Put your coat over a puddle so she can walk across it.

I'm just screwing with you. Don't do this. You'll ruin your coat and prove you're an idiot.

Always let her order her meal first.

Don't order her meal for her unless you're ordering the 2-for-$20 deal at Applebee's. If you order for her, it makes her look powerless in the relationship. If she doesn't know what she wants, wait for her to decide unless she tells you to order first. Then order the 2-for-$20 deal because you pretty much get an appetizer for free, and you can't beat that nowadays.

HOLD HER HAND

Walking through a mall. Entering the grocery store. Talking a walk through the city. Losing your balance and falling off a bridge.

Hold her hand. If you're falling off a bridge, make sure she goes with you. Dying alone would suck.

Holding the woman's hand shows her you're not embarrassed to be seen with her. You're proud of your relationship and—more importantly—it makes her feel like you're not trying to look single or in a friend-zone so you can hook up with the hot chick walking toward you in the Target parking lot.

Ladies, this works when you initiate it as well. Reach for his hand or take it when he offers. There's nothing more romantic than a couple holding hands for no reason other than they're together. Unless we're talking about old people. Really old people are gross.

If you offer your hand, ladies, and he doesn't take it or tells you his hands are dirty, check to see if there is an attractive woman approaching. If there is, he's thinking about nailing her and doesn't want to look like he's taken.

I can feel all the guys telepathically calling me "asshole" right now.

Go ahead, I can take it.

Act 2 Progress Checklist

Wow, it really looks like we've got the ball rolling right now and things are coming along. Hopefully, the ladies out there have caught their breath after seeing those pictures of me giving the sexy looks. Guys, if your woman read that last chapter and hopped all over you like virgins hop on Comic-Con tickets, you're welcome.

	Yes	No
Sexy looks, if done right, can be foreplay.	✓	☐
I would look good as a woman.	☐	✗
A woman biting her lip = boner time.	✓	☐
A woman biting *your* lip = bigger boner time.	✓	☐
You should notice the little things about your partner.	✓	☐
I'm a total dickhead for not realizing my girlfriend only had nine fingers.	✓	☐
After your woman gets into the car, slam the door on her foot to show her it's real.	☐	✗

Act 3 - Finders Keepers

I. Gone Fishin'

setting, and the theater curtains open to show our hero
... very end of a dock. He is wearing a flannel shirt, a
... shorts because he's an idiot. Someone please tell this
... sty—

Wait. Forget it. It's just regular pants that are rolled up so they don't get wet. Carry on.

On the dock lies this very book, open with a bookmark resting on this very page. This is kind of freaky when I think about it because I'm typing this page right now, so it's almost like I'm changing history.

man jumps into water but can't swim and starts drowning

giant eagle swoops down, clutches him from certain death and returns him to the dock

Mila Kunis runs by topless, holding a sign that reads, "I love Rodney"

Okay. That was pretty cool. SUCH POWER I WIELD.

The man reaches down and grabs his fishing pole from the dock. He sighs and looks dismayed, probably because he realizes he's fishing and forgot to bring a six-pack. Luckily for him, I haven't finished writing this page so—

16 Hooters girls show up with a keg of beer

He pours himself a big cup, takes a long sip, wipes his upper lip, and sets the beer down beside the book. Picking up the book, he thumbs back through the pages making sure he has everything he needs to proceed with Act 3.

"The Look," he says to himself, giving that sly wink and a nod toward the audience.

Several females and one guy sitting alone in the 15th row get flustered.

"Check," he says as he flips a page.

Turning back toward the audience, he singles out an attractive woman on the front row. She's sitting with a man picking his fingernails.

"Hey," he says to her. "Weren't you in here last week? You sat two rows back and had on a purple outfit. Is your headache any better? I remember you rubbing your temples a bit."

"Why, yes," she replies, stunned. "I was here, and I feel better, thank you."

She stands up and makes her way to the stage and hands him a piece of paper. It's a phone number and the words "Call me" scrawled across the top and underlined. Three consecutive Xs finish the note.

"What was that about?" the woman's husband asks as she returns to her seat.

"Nothing," she replies.

"Your nipples are hard."

"I'M COLD."

The man on stage looks down at the book again.

"Notice things about them," he says to himself. "Check."

He turns to put the book down and his gaze falls upon the rear of the theater. He freezes. With a jolt, he launches to his feet and leaps off the stage. He stumbles slightly as he lands, but he collects himself and rockets up the aisle. The audience follows him as he bear-tackles a man walking in.

"Johnny!" a woman screams.

A struggle ensues in the middle of the theater; there is yelling and commotion. No punches are thrown, but there's a lot of wrestling and grunting noises. Tufts of cotton fly out from the scuffle in every direction.

After another few seconds, our hero stands over the tackled man, a destroyed teddy bear in his hands. He looks at the woman who just screamed.

"I'm sorry, ma'am," he says. "But he was about to give you this." He holds up the partially stuffed animal. It's missing an eye.

She glares at the man on the theater floor who was about to give her a ginormous 4-foot tall teddy bear. She looks up at our hero.

"Thank you," she says. "You've saved me."

"It was nothing," he replies. "Any gentleman would do the same."

A Pegasus swoops in and flies him back to the stage while The Scorpions enter the orchestra pit and begin playing "Rock You Like a Hurricane"

Okay, seriously, this is pretty frigging cool.

Satisfied that he is ready, the man sits back down on the dock. He pats the book lying beside him, grabs his fishing rod, and casts his line into the waters of Lake Relationship.[1]

Silently, patiently, he waits for a nibble.

Bigfoot, wearing a leather bodysuit, waves 'hello' from behind a tree

Damn, that's cool.

---

[1] I need to apologize for the fishing analogy here. I don't want you to think I'm calling the women out there 'fish', and by doing so, referring to you as something men just wait to catch. I also don't want you to think I'm maybe talking about vaginas or something. More than likely, you didn't see that last metaphor until now, so maybe I shouldn't have even said it.

II. The "F" Word

"Flowers always make people better, happier, and more helpful; they are sunshine, food, and medicine for the soul." — **Luther Burbank**

"Mammals, a day of reckoning is coming. That's right, the same plants and flowers that saw you crawl from the primordial soup will reclaim the planet. And there will be no one to protect you." — **Poison Ivy**

Man, that Poison Ivy lady is a nutjob.

I titled this entry "The 'F' Word," but in this case the "F" word I'm talking about is "flowers." You people are twisted. I know what you were thinking (I was, too, but don't tell anyone).

Sending someone flowers is a little different than the chocolates or teddy bear no-nos previously mentioned. For example, flowers tend to make things brighter and prettier, while chocolate can kill a dog if ingested. By the same token, flowers can reflect the beauty of the woman you love, while teddy bears eat the souls of children.

Your move, loverboy.

Ladies, this tip may work the very first time you send your man flowers because WHAT MAN GETS FLOWERS? None, really, so (a) you have the element of surprise, (b) he will be absolutely floored at the gesture (what man doesn't like to lose the upper hand in a relationship once in a while?), and (c) the man will then feel obligated to get you something in return.

However, if your man enjoys getting flowers on the regular, you may have larger relationship issues than you know. I'm just saying there's a reason why you've found him looking in the mirror on more than one occasion, wearing your new pumps, and calling himself "Ms. Louise Titmacher."

Ah, flowers. I'm not talking "Valentine's Day" flowers or "Anniversary Bouquets" here. I'm talking about sending her flowers in the middle of the week just because.

The key here? JUST BECAUSE.

What says "romance" like a dozen long-stem roses coming out of the blue besides, literally, saying the word "romance?" Not much.

If your relationship is in the flower-giving stage (i.e., you both mutually like each other or have been married for 20+ years or your spouse just died and you need something to put on the casket), then flowers are a great way to say, "I'm thinking of you for absolutely no reason other than I'm thinking of you."

Tricks to this method:

The most effective way to get every ounce of romance from this gesture is to send the flowers to her workplace *in the middle of the day*.

Sending flowers to her job will catch her off guard. Additionally, you'll get the all-important "wow factor" from her coworkers and—even better—it will make them jealous.

Jealous coworkers are awesome because when you pick her up from work or drop by for lunch, you'll have their adoration. And those jealous female workers will go home and mention to their husbands or boyfriends that "so-and-so got flowers delivered today for no reason," thus making their men look bad which simultaneously makes you look better.

Sending her flowers at work also has the added benefit of marking your territory without you having to pee all over her desk or cubicle. Most employers frown upon this. Take my word for it. It's a win for everyone.

If you send flowers to her work, make sure you have the address handy and that she's actually going to be there.

I once sent flowers to my wife on a day when she was working at a different office branch and then spent the next hour scrambling for addresses to reroute the delivery truck. It was exhausting, and flower delivery people don't have the great sense of humor you think they'd have.

I don't know why I think flower delivery guys have a sense of humor except that I can't think about the word "bulb" or "fiddlehead" without giggling, so I assume florists must laugh constantly.

Sure, roses are romantic, and violets are fat gum-chewing kids that turn blue and roll around chocolate factories, but the words accompanying the flowers are what get the job done. A good note choice for the first dozen roses you send to someone is simply, "Just thinking about you."

WARNING: Do not send flowers that say "Thinking about you" if the date went terribly wrong or water was thrown, because stalking is not caring.

Back to the note and what it should say. Take, for instance, these examples of flowers I've sent in the past.

Take this card to the right, for instance.

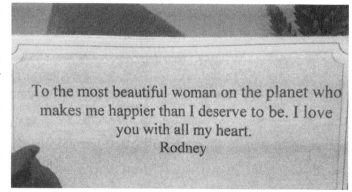

OH MY GOD I just got heart palpitations reading that card, and I'm the one who sent it.

Here's another one:

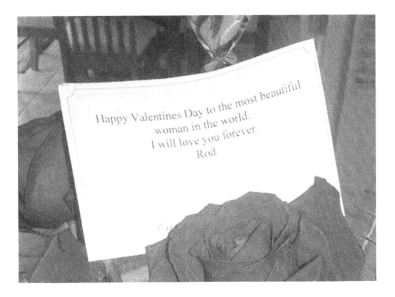

Please take note of the extensive use of the term "beautiful" here. This is some foreshadowing of my later section on dishing out compliments. See? *It all ties together*, which is what I think I'll title my book on advanced bondage techniques.

You can even turn explosive diarrhea into a charming, tender moment. Observe:

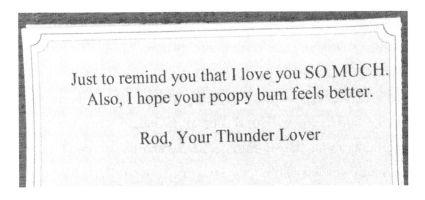

That one was really fun narrating to the lady taking the flower order, especially when I had to spell out "poopy" for her. Spelling is very important on a card accompanying a bouquet of roses, even if it's about your woman having a bad case of the Hershey squirts[1].

One more:

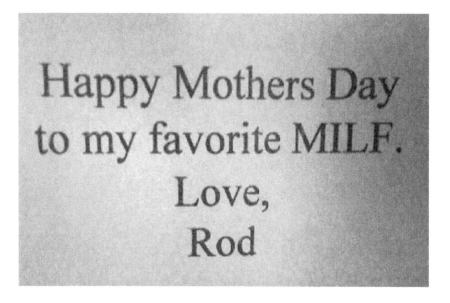

The genius of this is that it hit on several levels, since it was, in fact, Mother's Day, and my wife is a MILF. Actually, for me she is a MIDF, but that's beside the point, plus "MIDF" is really hard to say without sounding like you're having a stroke.

You: You're my favorite MID ... MIDduff ... MIDFFF ...

Florist: SOMEONE CALL 9-1-1!

Additionally, there is the key component of humor in the last card, giving it not only the *awww* factor but the *ha* component as well. If you can work such dual-magic into the card while not being completely embarrassed as you dictate it to the florist, you will hit this on all cylinders. Trust me.

Here's the thing about flower cards: They're short. You don't have to write an 8-page single-spaced soliloquy. The florist won't let you anyway. The floral industry imposes a character limit on you.

You get to be a guy and not say much, and she can't complain about your

---

[1] TIP: Make sure your significant other appreciates your jokes before sending flowers to her workplace that mention her inability to produce solid stool or the appearance of a hemorrhoid.

lack of elegant prose because of some federal florist card regulation. It's completely out of your hands.

See? Brilliant.

If executed properly, you may get something like an instant message popping up on your computer, gushing about the gesture, like this:

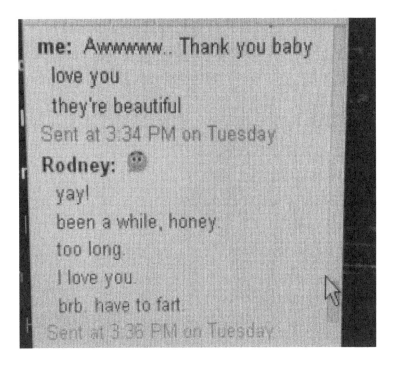

You should leave out the part about farting. I'm a trained professional, and this type of response takes years of practice.

FOR THE LADIES Prologue:
This Rose Is Making Me Thorny

My friend, Julie, had a great idea for any woman thinking of sending flowers to her man. I didn't think I could paraphrase it any better than how she wrote it, so I'm including it here in its entirety. This also means that I am not responsible for any terrible grammar contained between the quotes. Here goes:

"I sent a dozen roses to my boyfriend's workplace with a note attached to the stem of each one. The notes consisted of complimenting him on his oral game; thanking him for putting down the toilet seat after he pissed; and not complaining when one of my hairs ended up in the dinner I cooked. Of course, men being men, his co-workers read all the notes as well. They thought it was hilarious and my praise of his sexual prowess earned him major props."

That's pretty awesome. If you're going to send flowers to a man, ladies, this would be how you do it. I don't suggest sending something like this if he works in the Human Resources Department, though. Home Depot? Sure. Go for it.

This would also work as a great idea if you want to send flowers to yourself just to get the attention of someone else.

"Rodney, you are an amazing lover."

"I can't believe I had 38 orgasms last night."

Thanks for the tip, Julie!

Hmm. Maybe "Thanks for the tip" could be another thing you ladies could put on the card ...

III. Even a Blind Squirrel Finds a Nut Once In a While

I thought I'd title this story with one of the worst sayings known to man. I highly doubt there are a lot of blind squirrels out in the wilderness, but even if that's so, my guess is that they would have been picked off early in their lives.

Squirrel #1: JIMMY! LOOK OUT!

Squirrel #2: Who's there?

Squirrel #1: It's Sal—YOU NEED TO RUN!

Squirrel #2: Oh, hey Sa—

hawk scoops up blind squirrel as a tiny cane and pair of sunglasses fall to the ground

Squirrel karma sucks.

My point is that sometimes things fall into your lap. Hopefully these things aren't heavy or pointy, because maybe you want children one day. I have no idea. If you are considering children, give me a call so I can talk you out of it.

Just kidding (not really).

Armed with the knowledge gained earlier, your search for a new relationship may begin with hope and resolve. This will go away shortly, when you realize that most people you approach have something seriously wrong with them.

Usually, this is some type of clinical disorder that isn't yet categorized by modern medicine. Other times, they're New York Yankee fans. Whatever the turn-off is, you may find you're waiting a little longer for that love nibble[1] than you thought you would.

It's then, with hopes dashed and your guard down, that someone special comes into your life. If your guard is down, it may also be when you are mugged on a street corner and left for dead, so always remember to stay alert and aware of your surroundings. Just because you're looking for love doesn't mean you shouldn't stay vigilant.

I consider "going off on a tangent" a large part of my cardio routine.

Back to the unexpected relationship ...

The year was 1987 ...

I was almost 21 years old and spent the majority of my time hanging out at a nearby beach with my friend, Jeff, trying to score with chicks. Jeff was way better looking than I was, so I had to compensate for my stature and boyish looks by having a spectacular mullet, wearing acid-washed jeans, and tanning three days a week.

Oh, laaaaaaddiiiiiiiieees.

I was attending a local college at the time, and in a drunken stupor at a Thursday night dorm party, I decided that going from the third floor to the second could be done much more efficiently if I jumped out of a window instead of using the stairs. In related news, my parents wasted a lot of money providing me with a higher education.

When I leap from the third floor, I thought, *I'll land on top of the entranceway roof. Then I'll waltz in through the second floor window.*

In my head, this was a much better plan than walking down twelve steps. So, I leaped, or leapt. Whatever.

FYI, this would be a great place to stop and talk to your children about

---

[1] "Love nibbles" are now officially the name of my signature sex move. You are not allowed to use it unless you're shouting at me, "Just do the love nibbles, already. I'm tired and have to get up early for a dentist appointment."

alcohol and its direct relationship to idiocy.

I can still hear both my ankles snapping as I landed on top of the entranceway. If you've ever eaten a hard pretzel, think of biting into one that is roughly the size of Kansas, and you've got the appropriate sound effect. I ricocheted off the little rooftop and landed sideways in the bushes below, where of course, I added a cracked rib to my broken ankles.

Jack Daniels: 1

Rodney Lacroix: 0

Four weeks later, with shin-high casts on both legs and hindsight laughing at me from my peripheral vision, I was pretty depressed. To ease me out of my funk, Jeff suggested we take a trip to the beach, because what could be more fun than walking in sand with a pair crutches, right? Right.

After hobbling around the strip for five minutes, I was exhausted. I don't even like walking to my car, so the extra exertion was killing me. We took a break and sat on the seawall, facing the strip and making fun of people. We were young, and that's what young people do, because they're unaware they're complete assholes.

A big, white convertible stopped in front of us. The four girls inside yelled in our direction.

Hot Girls: C'mon! Get in!

Jeff glanced at me and motioned to get my ass off the wall. Not wanting to play a crippled-reptile version of *Frogger*, I shook my head "no." So Jeff did what any other guy would do in this situation: he slid off the wall, jumped into the car, and rode away, cackling and giggling with the carload of females.

I have terrible friends.

Jeff never looked back as the car pulled away. I can still picture myself sitting on that wall alone[1], watching the convertible disappear and wearing the same expression as a caged puppy in an ASPCA commercial. The main difference here is that in this version of the ad, the puppy also has broken feet.

runs off to adopt puppy

I sat there alone for what seemed like forever, imagining Jeff returning with his clothes torn and body lipstick-smeared. He would sit beside me and regale me with tales of orgies and fig leaves and grapes and people in clown masks.

I don't know how group sex works.

That's when I heard it:

> "That poor guy! He looks so sad and all alone. Let's go talk to him and cheer him up."[2]

I looked up to see two women crossing the street. They were doing a much better job with the traffic than I would have done, mainly because their limbs weren't shattered. They stopped in front of me and rattled off questions:

Woman 1: What happened?

Woman 2: Why are you so sad?

Woman 1: Why are you alone?

Why am I alone? Good question. I fantasized that somewhere out there, at that very moment, Jeff was being assaulted in the butt with fig leaves by

---

[1] And now, thanks to the magic of my illustrator, Noreen Conway, you can see it too.
[2] 80% of all porn starts this same exact way. Sadly, this was one of the 20% times.

clowns eating grapes.

I looked at these two women who were so concerned with my well-being that they went out of their way to come talk to me. I sat upright, smiled a dimpled smile, adjusted my crutches against the wall, and said the first thing that came to mind:

Me: So ... which one of you wants my number?

Surprisingly, one of them did. Sometimes, bad pickup lines are the best ones. I'm still not sure if it was the sympathy vote, my fantastic mullet that curled a little when it got too long, or the fact that these women knew I couldn't chase after them, but you know what? I threw out a line and it worked.

Stranger still, the relationship that resulted from this fiasco was one of the longest I've ever had in my life.

The moral of this story is:

Even when you're not looking for love, good things can happen to you. It's that blind-squirrel-finding-a-nut analogy, but in this case, it was a squirrel who drank too much and did something really stupid that busted both his ankles.

The secondary moral of the story is:

Abandoning your crippled friend on a seawall at the beach so you can run off with a carload of girls in an attempt to get laid ... may result in you getting mononucleosis.

Squirrel karma might not be so bad, after all.

IV. The "Funny Truth" Tip

"For me, the most attractive thing in a man is the ability to make me laugh." — **Mollie King**

"It's always funny until someone gets hurt. Then it's just hilarious." — **Bill Hicks**

Here's the situation:

You're in the bar, or maybe suffering through a friend's wedding (or more likely, at a bar at a wedding because weddings suck and people keep trying to make you dance). Or maybe you're doing one of the 37 people-searches you do every single hour on Match.com *(refresh – nope, refresh – nope, refresh – GAH, is that a Yeti?, refresh – nope ...)*.

There, in front of you, is someone you sense you can make a connection with.

> **TIP: If you're at a strip joint and sense this, flee immediately because you're about to lose $700 on lap dances. Trust me.**

Maybe it's how that person looks or something he said in his profile that made you smile unexpectedly. Maybe her online profile pic is just a shot of some amazing cleavage, or it's a guy who shaved his stomach hair to look like a six-pack (a clear indication that the man may, in fact, be a genius).

Now what? What do you do? How do you proceed?

You don't know how to juggle Chihuahuas, so how can you make the other person interested in you? More specifically, how can you make them interested in you without them finding the bouncer, drowning you in pepper spray, or canceling their home internet service and living out their remaining days alone in a mountain cave talking to a rock they've named Mr. Crunchington?

HINT: Attempting to juggle Chihuahuas will cause the latter reaction. Don't ask.

Now let's say you're already in a relationship. Luckily for you, that means you're already past the above stage and have managed to hook that special someone.[1]

How you did it is unimportant for this chapter *(if it's Chihuahua juggling, please contact me directly because I need to know your secret).*

And for argument's sake, let's assume it's not like how most of my relationships started, with a promise of a promotion in the company.

Either way, the main point here is that there is a connection, and for that bond to grow, it needs sustenance. Like a plant needing water or a Kardashian craving paparazzi, there has to be continued support for a relationship to flourish.

It's no secret that humans value a sense of humor above almost all other traits—including attractiveness—when choosing a mate. I would cite several examples that I Googled to support this fact, but I hate sharing credit with others.

So if you can make a prospective mate—or your current one—smile or laugh, then you've got your foot in the door. If you already had your foot in

---

[1] Please note my crafty use of "hooking someone" as it relates to the guy fishing in this section's opening dialogue. Also please note that "hooking someone" is different than "hooking for someone" as my parole officer has told me multiple times.

the door, then you have, like, up to your calf in the door, or maybe mid-thigh or something. I don't know.

As an example, the following is the true story of how my wife and I met ...

I was recently divorced and decided to take my search for a relationship to the Internet. This led me to several websites which got me in a lot of trouble with the Human Resources Department and also maxed out most of my credit cards. You'd be amazed at how quickly $19.99/minute charges can add up.

I joined one of the more popular dating sites, and began the process of building the most perfect profile one could ever imagine (if you've read my first book, **Things Go Wrong for Me**, you can see the profile in its entirety). Here are some simple excerpts from the profile:

> STOP!!! Looking for tall, dark and handsome?! Well...honestly...that's kind of a bummer.

As you can see, in my opening profile section, I have some honesty and humor. A lot of people online tend to embellish in regards to body type, height, weight, interests, allergies to pets, lack of felony convictions, etc.

For Internet dating, this has the unwanted effect of the "WTF FACE" when you finally meet someone.

> **Them:** WTF. You said you were in "average shape." You're not even close. An average shaped person only needs one chair. By the way, you have a leftover chunk of donut stuck to your cheek.

Meeting someone in person or online requires honesty. Remember that at some point, if it works out, they're going to discover if you're lying or not. If you're okay with that, then I guess yay for you and enjoy crashing weddings as a career.

But out of the gate in my case, prospective women knew that I wasn't tall or dark, and I was more Carol Channing than Channing Tatum.

If they're looking for a tall, tan Channing Tatum, then they don't have to waste their time. This also explains why the guy with the profile name "Tall-Tan-Tatum" was so successful at online dating.

About me and who I'm looking for

If you're looking for tall, dark and handsome, I think I can give you that as long as you can settle for short, white and "I've seen worse."  ← the 'hook'

I live for my two kids, and pride myself in never wanting to let them down. I get along amazing with them because, honestly, we're roughly on the same maturity level. 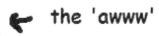 ← the 'awww'

If you're looking for a man who can have an in-depth, serious discussion about the Middle East and the economic impact of pork belly futures then keep moving..because this whole time that you've been talking, I've been thinking about last night's Family Guy. ← the 'funny'

My friends would call me funny, and I love being able to make people laugh. At 5'4" on a good day, I need every advantage I can get.  Intermission

So, yes, I did get quite a lot of feedback on my profile and talked to[1] or met[2] a number of women. But chemistry is chemistry, and we all can't be perfect chemists like the inventor of Flubber.

Sometimes, when things don't work out, you have to keep throwing your line back into the dating pool until you catch a decent fish you want to spend the rest of your life with. In Louisiana, the preceding sentence may not be metaphor.

Eventually I began custom searches for women because the same ones kept popping up in my results. Most of these recurring results did not seem

---

[1] Had coitus with.
[2] Had extra coitus with.

interesting to me (see my "Yeti" comment from earlier), so I expanded my search parameters a bit. The big part of this was to increase the height criteria of the man *she* was looking for.

My original setting for *"She is seeking a man"* was set between *5'2" tall to 5'5" tall* (which is where I and most of Snow White's dwarf friends fall). I changed this to *"5'5" tall to infinity,"* because it appeared that all women wanted a man who could see over a steering wheel without having to sit on couch cushions.

This is such bullshit. Have you ever heard that "good things come in small packages?" Maybe if it was "evil jerkwads come in tall packages," us short guys wouldn't get such a bad rap. If I seem bitter, it's because I am. Bitter things come in small packages, too. There, tall people, add that to your hate mongering agenda.

So, yes, I changed the height requirement to something I did not meet. This way I could maybe wear boots or inserts or some sexy spiked heels or something to make up the difference.

Honestly, I'm not sure what I was thinking.

I ran a new search with the height change.

There, lo and behold, on the very first page was this profile picture:

I died laughing for five minutes, because amidst the ridiculous selfies and duck faces and glamour shots that had been posed and reposed and retouched and filtered was this hysterical picture of Susan Boyle.

I opened the profile and saw the woman's height requirements for men:

> 5'9" tall to 6'4" tall.

Sonofabitch.

I was literally 6 inches shorter than her minimum requirement. If I stood up really, really straight, it only got me to within 5-7/8" of her minimum. My heart sank as I looked through her portfolio AND OH SHE IS CUTE, but still, I'd be a tough sell at 5'3" for a woman looking for a 5'9" guy.

I responded to her profile with the following:

> Hi,
>
> I saw your profile and damn near died laughing. I'm extremely way out of your height requirement at 5'3" but am willing to wear the heels in the relationship. Regardless, I just wanted to let you know that you made me laugh, so thank you.

She replied back and we began talking on a regular basis, most of which can't be rewritten here unless I want this book to end up in the erotica section.

gets idea for next book and starts writing screenplay with tall, tan Channing Tatum in mind for the leading character

And that's how I met my wife, Kerri.

Humor and honesty go a long way in creating and maintaining a relationship, even if you're well outside someone's ridiculous height requirements.

Seriously, give the little guys a chance, ladies, because we can be pretty damn nimble.

That said, I don't have to tell the guys out there to give tall or short women a chance because men will try to nail just about anything.

V. Wall Flowers

If you read my last book, **Perhaps I've Said Too Much**, you know that one of the greatest joys I have in life is masturbating.

Wait. Sorry. That's my first book.

In my second book, I dedicated an entire chapter to conversations I've had with Kerri over messaging and social media during the full course of our relationship.

This book is no exception because (a) it shows what being truly compatible with someone looks like, even over an Internet connection, and (b) it takes up space. To show you what that looks like, here are some of our better messaging sessions:

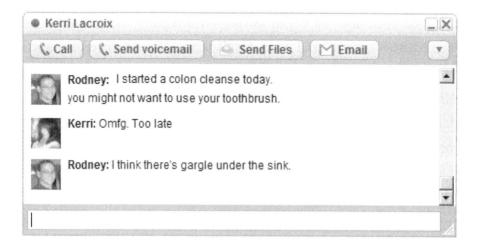

I think I found me a winner.

But, no matter what level you are in your relationship (unless it's Level 3 and you've had to register with your town), here is a fast and easy tip to show someone you're thinking about them at any time of day for any reason: randomly assault their Facebook page with loving messages.

NOTE: Pretty sure this violates a few laws, so proceed cautiously and/or maybe consult your lawyer.

Who doesn't like to get notifications from Facebook that the person you're dating or married to has just posted on your wall? No one. That is, unless the notifications are that your wife just sent you three pigs in Farmville or something. Seriously. Three pigs? I NEED CARROTS, WOMAN. It's like she doesn't even care about my harvest, sometimes.

Our marriage is a sham.

If you're sending your significant other lives in Candy Crush every four minutes, two things are likely going to happen:

1. You're going to be blocked, because that's easier than trying to figure out how to shut game notifications off. Thanks, Mark Zuckerberg.
2. You will be asked to find a job and help contribute to the family unit. Seriously. Who has time to play this much Bubble Witch Saga at 10:30 in the morning? GO DO SOMETHING PRODUCTIVE BECAUSE WE HAVE BILLS.

Every once in a while, I'll stalk my wife's Facebook page and see what she's up to. This is usually right after I send her three pigs in Farmville at 10:30 AM.

But while I'm on there, I like to remind her how I feel about her. As an example, I write things on her wall like, "You're beautiful," or "I am crazy about you," or sometimes I'll post stuff like this:

Rodney Lacroix
To my beautiful, Kerri. I love you so much, honey, that I wrote you this song just now.

Rod
~~Journey~~

Oh ~~Sherry~~ **Kerri** lyrics

~~Steve Perry~~

You should've been gone **to work**
Knowing how I made you feel
And I should've been gone **to the gym**
After all your words of steel
Oh I must've been a dreamer
And I must've been someone else
And we should've been over **easy eggs**.

    Kerri
Oh ~~Sherry~~, our love
Holds on, holds on
Oh **Kerri**, our love
Holds on, holds on

But I want to let go **of the riding crop**
You'll go on hurtin' me **yay!**
You'd be better off alone **with FaceBook**
If I'm not who you thought I'd be

But you know that there's a fever
Oh that you'll never find nowhere else
Can't you feel it burnin' on and on :)

    Kerri
Oh ~~Sherry~~, our love
Holds on, holds on
Oh **Kerri**, our love
Holds on, holds on

Go ahead. Try it. Just don't use this song, I have it copyrighted.

UPDATE:

It's Valentine's Day, 2015, as I type this particular page.

To go along with this section, I just received a notification that Kerri posted something to my Facebook wall. Here you go:

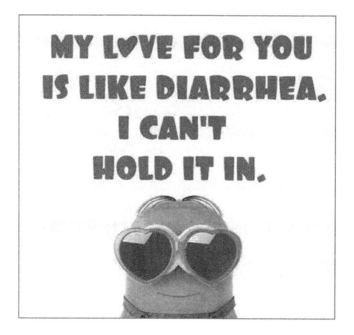

It's no song, but I think it gets the point across.

Act 3 Progress Checklist

Now we're really cooking. Actually, we really might be cooking because I smell onions. Hold on, I just forgot to put on deodorant this morning so false alarm on the cooking, there. This is what you get when I free-type whatever I'm thinking instead of putting together a cohesive thought. You can only imagine what happens at work when we hold brainstorming sessions. I get called to Human Resources a lot.

	Yes	No
Flower delivery, if executed properly, can be the exception to the rule of mundane gifts.	✓	☐
Women love it when you reference their intestinal distress on flower cards.	✓	☐
Jumping out of a window is a brilliant idea.	☐	✗
Chicks dig guys with broken feet, a tan, and a mullet.	✓	☐
You should always be serious in a relationship, even if your partner farts in her sleep.	☐	✗
You should only use social media for secretly trying to bang old classmates.	☐	✗
Susan Boyle saved my life.	✓	☐

Entr'acte #1

My fans list some romantic things that don't need to be treated with penicillin

The Fans Speak – Part 1

I have to preface this section by first stating that I had to look up "entr'acte" before using it as a title. This is not an intermission, but instead, some anecdotes related to the theme of the book. All of these tidbits would have been homeless if the French had not invented this term which means, "Between the acts."

Thank you, French people.

On most Saturday nights, my entr'acte usually involves having another drink, making sure the bedroom door is locked, adjusting my gimp mask, and trying to catch my breath.

So, there's some insight into what goes on at my house on the weekends.

I have a couple thousand Facebook friends (excluding my mother, for obvious reasons) and a few thousand Twitter followers (you can find me at @moooooog35, and if you want the story of THAT you'll have to get my first book). Normally, having that number of followers is something to brag about. That is until you realize Wendy's Baconator Twitter account has 36k followers, and it's a friggin hamburger, for Christ's sake. A delicious, delicious hamburger, but still ...

I posed the question on my media pages:

> "What's the most romantic thing you've done, or that someone has ever done for you?"

Here are some of the answers I received:

> "I did something very romantic for my boyfriend. Before he moved in I gave him a photo album with a few pages made from the first few months of our

relationship. Then, every week on Monday, I would print out my favorite picture from our weekend together and send it to him in the mail. Do unto others as you would have others do unto you. Let's just say I'm expecting a karma tsunami eventually." —**Brandi B.**

"When we were dating, I used to text message my now husband with words from songs I thought were romantic or appropriate for whatever was going on. Think, 'You are my Sunshine' first verse. He now will share songs he thinks are romantic with me from YouTube like "God Bless the Broken Road." — **Laura J.**

"1) I let my wife shave my back. 2) I let my wife shave my front." — **Del R.**

"Months after our small wedding, I took the dress to a consignment shop to sell. There is no one less sentimental than I am. I just didn't see the point of keeping it knowing I'd never wear it again. (It wasn't a big expensive dress or anything.) He went and got it back from the shop and even now, going on 22 years later, that stupid dress is still taking up closet space on my side of the closet." — **Linda D.**

"Mowed my yard ... seriously." — **Julie D.**

"My husband bought a case of the shampoo and conditioner that was in our hotel bathroom after I mentioned that I liked them. He had to search online to find the manufacturer." — **Laura S.**

"I used to date a woman who would write and send me actual letters on a weekly basis. Hand written and mailed love letters telling me how much she loved me and all the things she appreciated about me that week. She also used to be terrible at picking out gifts for birthdays and holidays. So she'd make me bouquets out of fanned and folded money. I got to buy my own presents, she *got to be the origami queen and make something that could be considered a crappy gift (why anyone would think cash is a bad gift, I have no idea.) I thought it was terribly romantic and thoughtful that she would spend days folding money into a bouquet of roses or lilies or something for me."* — **Karoline L.**

"I randomly sext people in hopes of adding a little romance to their lives." — **Robert D.**

Thanks to my fans for providing all of these great ideas. Well, almost all of them are great ideas. If anyone receives random sext messages, you can thank Robert. The guy is obviously a giver.

Act 4 - Courting With Disaster

I. Please Undo This Rendezvous

Everyone returns to their seats after the entr'acte, a bit more knowledgeable in regards to the French language. Everyone is back, that is, except the guy who had the sausage sub from the sidewalk vendor before the show started. He's still in the bathroom, and from accounts of other guys hurrying out, it doesn't sound too good.

Been there, dude. I had Brussels sprouts three days ago and I'm stil—

We don't need to go there. I apologize.

lights dim

Gunfire cackles loudly while flashes of explosions, not too far off in the distance, light up the dark theater. Men can be heard screaming amidst the rat-tat-tat of the emptying clips of automatic weapons.

As the scenery expands, we see anti-tank barriers strewn with barbed wire scattered across the midnight battleground. Soldiers appear from foxholes dug into the dirt and fire ahead into the darkness.

Sergeant: GO GO GO. WE'VE GOT YOU COVERED!

Further down in the trench, a man appears. He's wearing some khakis and a polo shirt, and the aroma of Old Spice Cologne fills the theater. It's apparent that their weird, new commercials have sucked in at least one poor bastard.

As he climbs, he turns, reaches down into the foxhole, and pulls out an attractive young woman. The other men stop firing to attempt to look up the woman's skirt because even in the heat of battle men think with their dicks.

"GO!" the sergeant yells again.

The man and woman bolt, hand in hand, and make their way across the battlefield. Mortar explosions blast around them, but the guy went heavy on the cologne, so it's providing them with an invisible shield. Pretty cool if you think about it.

Amidst the cover fire, they reach their destination. It's a movie theater. The man looks above him and reads the marquee.

Man: *Bridget Jones's Diary*? Really?

Woman: Yep. And afterwards we'll go to that new vegan restaurant.

Ah. You understand the scene now. **Date night**.

The man reaches for his wallet, but as he is about to hand a $20 bill to the woman in the ticket window, he pauses.

Two hours of Renée Zellweger followed by a lentil salad?, he thinks.

He turns around, drops his wallet to the ground, and runs headlong into the friendly fire. A few rounds ricochet off of the Old Spice bubble, but he keeps on. Eventually it is weakened and a single bullet slips through, hitting him in the chest. Another hits his shoulder and a third rips into his breast pocket sending bits of Trojan condom, ribbed for her pleasure, into the air.

"CEASE FI—" a soldier begins to yell, but realizes this is what the man wants. He lowers his signaling arm, and loads another clip.

The man slumps to the ground, bullet-ridden and bloody. As his pupils begin to dilate, a smile appears on his face.

Sergeant: We did him a favor, boys. Not every date can go swimmingly. Sometimes, you do what you can and hope for the best. Other times, you just want to be put out of your misery.

The soldiers look at him.

Sergeant: What? *Swimmingly* is a word.

The soldiers stand up in their foxholes to see the woman entering the theater. She's carrying a big bucket of popcorn.

Vegans.

II. The List
(Not Schindler's, That Would Be a Downer)

The List can either doom or enhance a relationship. Hey, that makes me think of Dr. Doom, which makes me think of the guy from *Nip/Tuck* who played him in the movies. Now I'm thinking about sex scenes from the show, and I should seriously call my own doctor about getting a prescription for my ADD. I wonder if he can make protective shields like Dr. Doom can. Maybe Dr. Doom could only make protective shields because he wore too much Old Spice.

Yep. Totally asking for a prescription.

Where were we? Oh yes ...

The List always starts with a simple question: "Why do you love me?"

Oh boy.

It was late, and I had just finished *almost* satisfying The Woman (not Kerri). I say "almost" because things tend to come to a screeching halt when you accidentally blurt out "SCHENECTADY" during climax because you've been thinking about fun city names in a feeble attempt not to finish faster than a bull rider.

> **Me:** *stroking her hair*
>
> **The Woman:** *looking back at me longingly*
>
> **Me:** God, I love you.
>
> **The Woman:** Yeah? Why?

Sonofabitch.

If I'd had any flash grenades, I'd have thrown one behind her and escaped in a blanket of thick fog. But I'd used them all while practicing my guitar solo for "Careless Whisper" the night before.

The Woman stared and waited for an answer. A giant, burning light shined down upon me, and I felt pressed to list all kinds of things about *why* I was in love.

Of course, I had to come up with *original reasons* that didn't sound generic or lame like, "I love your eyes," or "I love you because you're funny" which would have been followed by her impression of Joe Pesci saying, "Oh yeah? Funny how? Like funny ha ha?"

I wished she'd broken out a baseball bat and beat me to death with it. Death can be a sweet, sweet release in situations like that.

Me: Why? ... Why not?

And that, my friends, is how not to respond.

Because I like my readers, I did a little research[1] and came up with some suggestions on how to avoid the breakup when you're faced with this harbinger of doom. Avoid answers like:

1. You have beautiful eyes.
2. You have an amazing smile.
3. You have ass dimples.

---

[1] No research whatsoever.

4. I am enamored by your ample melons.

   5. You're cheaper than most hookers.

Chances are your woman has heard them all when she was at the bar with her girlfriends last Saturday night, and that guy wearing the Affliction t-shirt and downing his fifth Red Bull hit on her.

There's a reason she (probably) didn't go home with the guy, so let's focus on some other things about her (or him, ladies—you can play, too) that show her you're really paying attention (even if you aren't).

Of course the caveat to this is that you've actually been paying attention, and if you haven't, shame on you.

That said, there is a way to avoid being taken off guard by this question when you're asked WHY at 11 PM, and all you want to do is go back to sleep. It's a mystery to me why women choose this time to discuss things that can't be resolved.

So, to cut your losses, here are some pointers to head this off at the pass.

Roughly eight weeks into dating Kerri, I wrote her an email.

Yes. Email.

The subject of the email was, simply "A list" and went something like this:

Scarlett Johansson

Jennifer Lawrence

Mila Kunis

Whoops. Sorry. That's from "*A-List* celebrities I'd bang." Different email conversation entirely. Here's the actual "A list" email to her:

Hi honey,

I was just sitting here thinking about you and things I love about you. Here they are, in no particular order.

- *Your Betty Rubble laugh*

- *You laugh at my jokes even when they're terrible*

- *You are an incredible mother*
- *The way you look at me with those amazing eyes*
- *You don't mind keeping your heels in the closet when we go out so I don't look even shorter*

YES. I realize I broke my own rule here by including her eyes, but in my defense my wife has incredibly beautiful eyes. If your significant other has a wonky eye or is cross-eyed or wears an eye patch, you may need to revise that line (i.e., *"The way you look at me with that amazing eye, I think. I'm not sure because it always looks to the right."*)

The key here is that you point out the little things about her. It's all in the details. The things she does every single day that endear her to you—that maybe no one has ever told her before—are the things that show her she is special to you.

The small birthmark behind her ear that looks like Mount Rushmore, perhaps, or the middle toe that's longer than the other. It sounds weird, but mention things she hasn't heard before or maybe doesn't notice herself. Do this, and you will touch her heart. Just don't try touching it by using that long gross toe of hers. She's getting kind of self-conscious about it at this point.

For parents: There is nothing hotter than a mom or dad who gives everything for their kids. I pay child support so I actually give everything I have plus an additional 33% that I can't even claim on taxes. Thanks, Uncle Sam. But if you're with a parent, make sure you let them know that you notice how awesome they are as a mom/dad—unless they actually suck at it. Then you should stick with the "long toe" thing.

Ladies: As men, we are always worried we aren't doing things right. Tell us how safe we make you feel or the way you feel when we kiss you, and we'll keep doing it. Tread carefully, though, because if you tell us we make you melt when we kiss you when in reality it's like being attacked by a hairy plunger, you'll become a victim of your lies, and you're in for some heavy plunger attacks on the regular. Heed my warning.

Moments after my wife received *The List* in her work email, she immediately replied, awestruck.

Relationship point scored! And most important, a future "Why do you love me" midnight ambush was successfully averted.

You know the question is coming at some point in the relationship. It always does. So take ten minutes and think about the *WHY* of it all, and surprise them with the list first.

Then throw out your Affliction t-shirt. Seriously, dude.

III. Uptown Girl Makes Downtown Boy Look Like an Asshat

"I would really love to see Billy Joel." — **My girlfriend, circa 1989**

They say that music can soothe the savage beast, so it's logical to assume that it can also appease your lady when you give her concert tickets. I apologize for referring to your mate as a "beast." I'm sure she's a very handsome woman.
throws smoke bomb and runs away
I really enjoy going to concerts and have instilled this same love into my children. I have also instilled in them the love of 1980s hair bands and heavy metal so I can buy tickets for concerts that I want to go to and bring them along. They think it's a present for them, when obviously, they're just talkative baggage for the evening.

Raise your children in this fashion, and you will never have to suffer through a One Direction or Justin Bieber concert. You're welcome.

Back in the 80s, I dated a girl who loved Billy Joel. It wasn't an issue for me, because "Glass Houses" was one of my very first albums—yes, albums—so I grew up listening to "You May Be Right" and "I May Be Crazy" and "You May Be Right, I May Be Crazy." I can't remember any of the other songs on that album, plus I'm padding my word count for this book.

As was my luck back then, Billy Joel came to Boston. Remember the quote at the beginning of this section? That, my friends, is a prime example of the age-old practice: "dropping a hint."

When your woman looks at you and says, "I would love to go to X," it is intended to be heard as "you should take me to X because if you don't take me to X, I will hate you forever."

As a romantic surprise for my girlfriend's birthday, I scored Billy Joel tickets for the Boston Garden. No boyfriend had ever bought her concert tickets as a present, and she said it was really thoughtful of me. In her defense, it *was* really thoughtful of me[1].

Our seats were about three miles from the stage, floor level, in front of the control booth. We were barely taller than five feet and everyone in front of us was the height of King Kong, so we had an amazing view of shirt tags and the party side of mullets.

I hate being short because it sucks 99% of the time. The other 1% of the time, it's okay, because my face is boob-level with taller women.

We had a decent time, laughing and singing and dancing, which was more perilous than it sounds because we stood on our seats the entire concert. It was our only way to see Billy Joel, assuming he was the ugly guy at the piano.

My girlfriend had a blast. I know this because she gave me that look that said, "I'm having a blast," and she may or may not have actually said "I'm having a blast" a few times. It was either that or "I have bad gas." I'm not sure. It was loud, and I'm terrible at reading lips.

"Man," I thought, "I really scored on this one. I'm gonna get soo ... sooooo

---

[1] This is one of those times where I hurt my shoulder trying to pat my own back. Additionally, my fingers were hurt as well. Not from typing, though ... from taking a writing break to practice my guitar. So I get it, Bryan Adams. I get it.

... oohhhhhh ..."

During my chair-dancing frenzy, I turned around in my seat and glanced over at the control booth just ten feet behind us. The control booth is where guys control the lights and sound and—in the case of Iron Maiden concerts—giant mummy-zombie-skeleton-things emerging from the backdrop.

It was there, amidst the men pushing buttons and sliding bars and turning knobs and widgets and kerbupples and other technical things that my gaze landed upon her: Christie Brinkley.

Did I forget to mention that at the time, Billy Joel was married to Christie Brinkley? If I did forget to tell you, please note this concert was shortly after Billy Joel married Christie Brinkley, thus cementing one of the weirdest couple mismatches in history. This includes the time I dated a really hot girl for two years who was 5 foot 10. It felt like being a little horny Jack and the Beanstalk.

But there she was, just a scant ten feet away from me. Christie Friggin Brinkley (not her real middle name, probably).

This was the same woman who adorned several posters hung above my bed at the time. She also appeared in several of my dreams, but you don't want to know the details, and I'm not going to write them because my daughter told me she wants to read this book when I'm done, and she needs enough therapy just being my daughter.

I remember it as though it was yesterday ...

Christie wore a white dress and

swayed back and forth to whatever the ugly bug-guy at the piano was singing. I was transfixed. I couldn't move. I stood there on my seat for what seemed an eternity, completely turned around, ogling my childhood dream girl ... a lovely vision in whi—

poke

poke poke

Something poked me. Cupid? Was it Cupid?! A tiny cherub launching love darts at my arm?!

I turned toward the poking to see my girlfriend staring at me with a very non-cherub gaze, and instead of her lobbing love darts at me, she shot daggers from her flaming eye sockets.

She was a bit peeved that I was turned completely backwards in my chair, ignoring the concert and drooling. Also, I may or may not have had wood.

I felt the stupid smile plastered on my face transform into what can best be described as the "Yes, Dear" face of married men. Maintaining eye contact with me, she circled her finger in the air—pantomime for "TURN. AROUND. NOW."

I gave one last glance at Christie—and maybe blew her a kiss—before succumbing to my girlfriend's will. I turned, reluctantly, and suffered through another bald-googly-eyed-man piano song.

Cheering erupted behind me and I turned reflexively to see Christie Brinkley descending the control platform toward the stage.

WAIT. Toward the stage? Is she ... OHMYGOD SHE IS GOING TO WALK RIGHT PAST ME HERE SHE COMES HERE SHE COMES!! I AM

SO EXCIT—

It's at this point, with my head turned completely around like a barn owl, that my balance decided it was taking a break. My body, sexy yet twisted, heaved backwards, my knees buckling over the back of the overpriced chair I stood upon.

I tried to spin back around to right my flailing body, but it was too late, and I did a weird sort of backflip into the aisle behind us. If you've ever flipped a Slinky down a set of stairs, you can successfully picture what was happening. My instincts took over, and out of sheer desperation, I grabbed for anything to save me.

Snatching a healthy chunk my girlfriend's hair, I continued my slow-motion descent to the cold, concrete Garden floor. If you're a fan of the movie, *Jaws*, then you're also familiar with the part of Quint's speech where he talks about being attacked by a shark, and all you hear is high-pitched screaming. It was similar to that, except the screaming was my girlfriend as I clenched her hair in my white-knuckled fist and dragged her over the back of the seats with me.

I hit the floor first, my wrist buckling under the weight of my tiny, yet somehow super-muscular body. Pain shot up my arm, and I would have screamed if my girlfriend's body hadn't landed directly on my face.

I grabbed my nose and pulled my hand away to find it covered with blood—the next day I would discover that my nose had been fractured, which can typically happen when a woman lands on your face from a four-foot drop.

Normally, I am quite fond of women landing on my face, but this proved to be one of the rare exceptions. I stared at my bloody hand for what seemed like an eternity before the realization set in: OH MY GOD CHRISTIE BRINKLEY IS STILL RIGHT BEHIND US.

I sat up—letting go of my girlfriend's hair as she lay sprawled next to me—and glanced around to find Christie sauntering up the aisle. She had somehow missed the carnival of horrors that just happened right in front of her, and now she was three feet away.

ONLY THREE FEET AWAY.

As God as my witness, I have no idea what came over me next. As Christie Brinkley, my teenage dream girl, passed beside me, I screamed out, "CHRIIIIISSSTIIIIEE!!"

I screamed it like I was falling off a cliff and Christie Brinkley was the only one who could save me (after she saved me, she would put on that awesome blue one-piece bathing suit with the open side, her hair all windy and stuff, and we would make sweet, sweet love on my waterbed as she fondled my mullet).

"CHRIIIIISSSTIIIIEE!!"

I screamed it as loud as I could, my ever-swelling wrist all flippity-floppity while I sat crumpled on the floor, my girlfriend lying unconscious next to me, maybe. I have no idea.

"CHRIIIIISSSTIIIIEE!!"

Christie jumped.

She put her hand to her heart, startled and scared to death. Then, she turned to find who the hell just gave her a coronary. I saw her look quickly to her left but miss seeing me because HELLO I'M DOWN HERE.

If I didn't have brain damage, I bet I would have said something like "Look, Christie. I've fallen for you," and then winked or something smooth like that. Then she saw me out of her peripheral vision, looking like a guy who normally would have required a chalk outline on the floor.

She turned and looked at me. RIGHT AT ME.

I waved. I waved with my good hand because my other one was badly sprained and hurt like a motherfucker.

She smiled that amazing smile of hers and waved back. AYFKM SHE SMILED AT ME?! WHOA, WAIT. SHE SMILED AT ME AND WAVED BACK?!

The smile on my face grew so big it wrapped the corners of my mouth all the way around to my spine. The top part of my skull flopped backwards and my upside-down gaze fell upon my girlfriend's not-so-amused face.

"She waved at me," I said to my unimpressed date. I was drooling a little.

"Are you seriously fucking kidding me right now?" she replied.

I don't remember the rest of the concert, or the night, for that matter, so despite the build-up for this story, the ending sucks.

I can tell you that all the "How was the concert?" questions ended in a story about how I scared the absolute shit out of Christie Brinkley, and even though I almost died, did I mention that she smiled and waved back at me?

And that marked the first and last concert that I ever took my girlfriend to. I asked her to go to a few concerts after that, but we never went. In retrospect, you can't really blame her for not wanting to go. Near-death experiences have turned many a person off of contemporary rock.

The point is, Christie Brinkley smiled and waved at me.

Even though I almost became crippled and took my girlfriend to Handicap Town with me, I'm not sure anything is ever going to get better than that.

Actually, does anyone know if Cheryl Tiegs is married to a musician? If so, I just may have to get tickets.

IV. Make Sure the Men Who Died in Hallmark Didn't Die in Vain

If you've taken any of my advice or hints so far, then you're most likely knee-deep in the adoration and devotion of your significant other. Either that, or your partner is starting to feel smothered and you've just received the "I think I need some space" talk, and now you're living in a YMCA telling a guy named "Sketchy Jim" how this book has ruined your life.

If you're in this latter category, I'm really sorry. I should have told you that all of these tips need to be spaced out over the course of several years and that there's a 98.7% chance that Sketchy Jim has head lice.

My bad.

This chapter is dedicated to those guys mentioned in the very opening of this book, the ones who wandered into a card store and eventually died of old age or sheer boredom. This is for you, my brethren. Sleep well, sweet angels ...

We all know that we could easily be one of those poor bastards. You know all those times you've scoured the Hallmark Store looking for just the right card, staring at wall after wall of cardboard poetry:

- For Her
- For Him
- For It (when you really can't tell)
- Husband
- Wife
- Wives (Utah only)
- Love, Etc., etc.

The card categories seem endless.

But the one category most men and women seem to neglect or pass is the **Just Because** section. Yes, there is a **Just Because** section.

If you knew that, then you're probably already aware of this quick and easy tidbit, so you can skip ahead to the other parts in the book that require credit cards. That said, I am not to be held responsible for any laughs you may have passed over by not reading this chapter. Laughter is supposed to decrease stress and slow the aging process, so if you pass over this section and find yourself freaking out about how wrinkly and ugly you are, don't say I didn't warn you.

Where were we? Ah ... there is a Hallmark section that contains cards for no defined occasions. Under normal circumstances, people are searching for cards related to typical celebrations: Anniversary, Birthday, Valentine's Day, Take Your Penis Out at Work Day, National Dress Your Dog Day (*every day at my house, FYI*) etc., etc.

Pretty much everyone in a relationship expects to get a $4.99 card that expresses how you feel written by a guy named Stan who sits around all day at a desk looking like this picture to the right.

In Stan's defense, he's pretty attractive even when he's in deep thought.

But what he or she isn't expecting to find is a card in their underwear drawer that reads, *"Just because I wanted to say I love you."* I've opened my lunch bag in the middle of a really shitty day to find a card that says, *"You mean everything to me."*

The fact that I wrote it myself is beside the point.

I've also opened my lunch bag to find a note that says *"Buy tampons"* because Kerri knows that's the best way to remind me to get stuff on the way home. This always ruins lunchtime for me.

NOTE: **Just Because** moments are special because they are unexpected. If you give your lover a card every Thursday, it kind of defeats the surprise aspect and becomes a routine.

Remember, you can't spell "routine" without "r-u-t," and ruts can be an enemy of romance and cars with low suspensions. A man in a leotard doing interpretive dance during a viewing of The Notebook is another enemy of romance, but that's a different book entirely, and in my defense, I didn't know putting a shot of vodka into a beer would have that effect on me.

A woman that I was involved in a long-distance relationship with used to send me random cards every couple of weeks.

straps 14 pillows to body and curls up in a defensive turtle position as Kerri pounds away at my limp body incessantly upon reading this

When your contact with someone is usually by phone calls, texts, and Skype conversations, it's an incredible feeling to find a card in the mail with a handwritten note inside. Even more spectacular is finding naked pictures inside the card. The best, though, is when the card containing naked pictures isn't from your Uncle Jim.

You don't need to live hundreds or thousands of miles away to have **Just Because** moments. In fact, that probably makes it a lot harder to put the note in underwear drawers, now that I'm thinking about it. Also, I need to buy underwear. I also need to buy tampons. Sometimes I wish Kerri would stop putting grocery reminders in my lunch, and stick to the lovey-dovey notes. I seriously hate the feminine aisle in the store. Gives me the heebies.

So put this book down right now, run to the store, and buy a card for the simple reason that it will make her smile at a time when she's not expecting it. That's an amazing thing to do for someone you love.

And while you're there, can you grab some tampons for my wife? I'll pay you back, I promise. Thanks.

V. Cats Were a Bad Idea

"No matter how much cats fight, there always seem to be plenty of kittens." — **Abraham Lincoln**

I really dislike cats.

If you're an avid reader of my blog or books, you already know this rant. I love dogs. I'm a dog person. In fact, here is a photo of me writing this section at 5:30 PM on a Sunday afternoon with my faithful little mutt sitting next to me, not mauling me or shitting in a box somewhere, like a cat would do:

He's so goddamn cute I can't stand it.

But not everyone is a dog person. There are those people out there who enjoy the company of cats more than dogs or—in most cases—other people. We call these people "evil," "hoarders," or "prime suspects."

As much as we dog people may dislike *cat people*, they are a functional part of the caste system and provide the knitting and crochet industry with a steady stream of customers.

After my first divorce (I say "first" here because I have no idea if my current bride will take kindly to some of these stories that don't involve her), I re-entered the dating scene. One of these dating scenes was directed by Martin Scorsese and starred Leonardo DiCaprio. It was a confusing time for me even though it was star-studded and received phenomenal reviews from critics.

My mind drifts sometimes.

One woman I dated happened to live about 800 miles away. Normally this is enough to put the kibosh on most prospective dates, but when you're a short, balding man in your 40s, any bite is a good bite. She was cute and funny and we got along great but ...

... but ...

She was a cat person.

*cue Psycho *shower music**

She wasn't *just* a cat person. She was a *repost-kitty-videos* and *send-me-cards-with-cats-on-them* and *every-phone-conversation-included-cats* type of cat person.

Normally, the Crazy Cat Lady thing is a deal-breaker for me, but please remember I was a short, balding, man in my 40s. I mean, ABC wasn't banging down my door to offer me the starring role in the next season of *The Bachelor*. I could deal with a cat person, right?

Sure, let's go with that.

The oddest part about dating this woman wasn't her being a cat person, it was that she was a cat person *without cats*. This made her a true cat-crazy cat person—someone who loved and desired a cat but was catless. Cat-free.

This is a statistical anomaly in the cat-loving world and only occurs with one of every three million cat people, and lo and behold, I had begun a long-distance relationship with one.

Yay me.

We dated for a very long time and with much success. I would visit her. She would visit me. I met her mother. She made me try sushi.

You could say the relationship had its ups and downs, with the down part of me eating raw eel. So, so gross. It's like ingesting sea boogers.

But, although tiring, the relationship seemed to be working. With that in mind, during one of her visits up north, I decided to make the grandest romantic gesture a man can make in this situation:

I drove her down to my local animal shelter to buy her a cat.

Hey, I know it's not a ring or anything, but a Calico has, like, ringworm or something, so it's close. I know almost nothing about cats except that I'm allergic to them.

Oh. Did I not mention that? Yes. I'm incredibly allergic to cats.

INCREDIBLY ALLERGIC.

You're realizing, at this point, that a man who is very allergic to cats and buys his girlfriend one isn't the smartest man in the world. And you would be right. You are, as they say, "righter than rain." I'm not sure where that saying comes from, or why rain is right all the time, but let's just say that rain and I have at least that one thing in common.

As we pulled into the animal shelter, her eyes widened.

> **Her:** Why are we here?

> **Me:** I think it's about time you had a cat.

Her eyes welled. Her face beamed. She hugged me, asking "ARE YOU SERIOUS?" about 300 times, and yes, I was serious. And as I was about to find out, also very, very stupid.

> **Her:** This is the most amazing thing anyone has ever done for me.

BAM.

We walked into the shelter and asked where the cats were. I'm not sure why we asked, because from the front corner of the building you could hear something that sounded like hundreds of babies being water-boarded echoing from somewhere in the back.

When Obi-Wan Kenobi said he heard millions of voices crying out in terror, I always imagine he heard the same sounds I heard coming from that cat room. So annoying. I have no idea how you cat people put up with that shit.

As we were about to enter the room, she looked at me.

Her: Um. Aren't you allergic?

You know that scene in *Frosty the Snowman* where he's about to bring Karen into the greenhouse because she's freezing to death, and she looks at him and says, "But you'll melt," and he says ...

Me: Only a little.

So Frosty goes in and ultimately sacrifices himself for the sake of Karen because the evil magician guy locks them in. This sends Karen, now warm and toasty, into a panic, and she kills herself by ingesting poison. Then Santa revives Frosty who awakens to see Karen dead. Horrified and heartbroken, he throws himself on a space heater as the camera pans away to an expanding puddle. I haven't seen this in a while and may be confusing it with *Romeo and Juliet* or *Home Alone 2,* but honestly, I like this ending better.

I found myself feeling the same way as Frosty: willing to sacrifice myself to make this woman happy. In this scenario, the role of the evil magician is played by the shelter worker who let us into the room. But there's no Santa to come rescue Frosty from the evil cats this time. Santa isn't real, kids. Evil cats, though, are very, very real.

We entered the room and there in front of me were walls and walls of cats. Mewing and meowing and looking upon me in clear disdain were *hundreds* of cats. As we walked past each one, we glanced at the paperwork.

Nope. Too old.

Nope. Too fluffy.

This one just sucked out my soul, so you know, NOPE.

Me: There's a Chinese testicle staring at me.

Worker: That's a hairless. They're supposed to look like that.

Me: Really? Gross. I would name him Smoothie McScrotum.

Like I said, I'm a dog person. A dog person who was starting to get itchy, and hey, is it getting hard to breathe in here?

As we wandered the stacks of cats (I'm coining this as "CatStacks" and working on trademarking it), nothing jumped out at us, thank Christ. I could see the happiness in my girlfriend's face melt into disappointment.

That's when we saw the **Cat Playroom**.

Amidst beds and tubes and walkways and scratchy things and random objects covered in carpet were about 50 free-range cats. It was like *Planet of the Apes*, but instead of primates with guns, it was tabbies and shorthairs and Persians. The only way that room could've been any worse for me was if tarantulas were riding the cats like little cowboys. It looked like Hell.

Me: We should get out of he—

She went in. Sonofabitch she went in.

I reluctantly followed and found myself engulfed in a sea of these creatures. Bouncing. Jumping. Sleeping. I felt like how Jane Goodall must feel amongst a community of chimps, but instead, she's allergic to them and they all want to eat babies because they're direct descendants of Satan.

As my girlfriend looked at each cat and stopped to pet them, my gaze fell upon a fuzzy black cat lying on his side in a bed. I don't know why, but he appealed to me, so I approached his little cubby and reached out to tickle his belly.

Now, as a dog person, I had no idea cats don't like this. If you're a dog person and feel like tickling a cat's belly, a word of caution:

CATS DON'T LIKE BELLY TICKLES.

My fingertips grazed the cat's fuzzy belly, and I gave two small little scratches and maybe even said "coochie coo—"

That's when he clamped down.

The cat's body closed upon my hand like a steel bear trap. His claws, hidden from view just a split second ago shot out like tiny little switchblade knives. His eyes rolled over black, and his fuzzy little black face went from "sleepy" to "I KILL YOU."

The claws dug in first, wrapping around my fleshy forearm and hand, tearing into my skin and hitting bone. His mouth opened, and six-inch mandibles of death—SIX INCH MANDIBLES OF DEATH, I SWEAR—pierced the meat of my hand. Then, as is the custom of most chupacabra, he let out a guttural ROOORRRRWWWRRRRR.

Me: OHMYGOD OHMYGOD HE'S GOT ME ARRGGHHH

I instinctively yanked my hand from the cubby hole with the beast still firmly grasped to the end of my arm like it was a giant, carnivorous, fuzzy lollipop. I shook my arm violently, trying to loosen its grip, but the demon only dug in deeper.

Me: MOTHER OF FUCK SHIT GOD FUCK OW SHIT

Three shelter workers burst into the room and tried to yank that damn thing off me as blood poured down my arm and puddled on the floor. My girlfriend stood there, in horror, watching me get devoured in front of her very eyes.

Me (screaming at her): WHY CAN'T YOU LIKE PUPPIES?!? IT'S KILLING ME!

Pain shot up my shoulder as he pierced a nerve in my arm. Another shelter worker appeared, and they all worked on each of the cat's limbs, trying to peel them from my body. I was quickly approaching blackout phase, when finally, he loosened his grip and was successfully removed.

If this was a movie, 48 hours later an alien would burst from my chest.

My girlfriend rushed me out of the shelter as quick as she could. My wounds were deep and serious, so when I got home, I did what most men would do in the same situation: I doused on hydrogen peroxide and called it a day.

My body weight tripled over the next two hours as my allergies kicked in full force. I began to resemble a corpse that had been floating in a river for six days. Here's a photo taken shortly after my allergic reaction hit 100%:

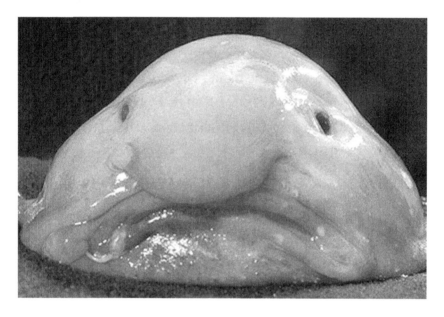

The next day, wounds untreated, I flew down with her to her hometown and stayed two days before deciding to call my doctor. My arm had turned into something that could best be described as *wicked scary looking*—hard, fat, and red, like a horny Santa.

The doctor told me I should go to an emergency room to have my arm seen, like, NOW. I hung up the phone, then drove myself one-handed to the airport and flew home, convinced I was slowly turning into a cat, and within a few days, I would be able to fall, unharmed, from ridiculous heights.

I went to the emergency room as soon as I landed. The diagnosis? *Acute cellulitis* in my forearm with a severe infection. According to the doctor, I was not turning into a cat, despite my newfound obsession with licking myself. The therapist he immediately referred me to said the same thing.

They put me on some pretty strong meds for the next two weeks and my hatred for felines increased tenfold, tempered only by the fact that my Tweets are ridiculous when I'm on painkillers. Every cloud has its silver lining, people, even if the cloud is near-dismemberment by a wirehair kitty.

Shortly thereafter, my girlfriend and I broke up. Long distances and life-threatening cat-attack arm infections can do that sort of thing to a relationship. As a word to the wise, I strongly recommend never, ever trying to give a cat as a romantic gift.

It's like that saying goes:

> *All things happen for a reason, and when the things that happen are bad, it's probably because of cats.*

Act 4 Progress Checklist

Wow. That section completely disturbed me.

Hopefully, your courtship goes a little more smoothly than the previous stories. Here are some things you can take away from this section without contracting cellulitis.

	Yes	No
Cats suck so bad.	✓	☐
Give your partner a list of things that you like about them.	✓	☐
When you make the above list, add their flaws in alphabetical order or in ascending order of grossness.	☐	✗
Buy cards for no reason other than saying, "I'm thinking of you."	✓	☐
Scaring celebrities is a great way to have sex with one.	☐	✗
Pay attention to hot, famous people instead of your date.	☐	✗
Cats are really the worst. This point cannot be emphasized enough.	✓	☐

Entr'acte #2

My fans list some UN-romantic things that don't need to be treated with penicillin

The Fans Speak – Part 2

Way back a bunch of pages I gave you some romantic responses from fans and friends when I posed this question on my social media accounts:

"What's the most romantic thing you've done, or that someone has ever done for you?"

I can tell you, not all the answers were heart-thumpers.

Here are some of the answers I got that fall less into the "Awww" category and more into the "Ewww" or "OHMYGOD" ones:

"On our 1st date, my husband tried to impress me with a lakeside picnic and champagne. The cork broke so he tried to break the bottle top off on some rocks. Cut the hell out of his hand, but damn if I wasn't impressed." — **Lisa Marie W.**

"Does holding my hair while I puke after a night at the bar count as romantic?" — **Jenny D.**

"While out strolling in the woods we came upon a small creek, not wanting for me to get my feet wet, he picked up a large rock (mmmuscle) to give me a stepping stone. As he dropped it in the water I got covered in mud!" — **Tonya M.**

"I had a bout of conjunctivitis during a romantic dinner. I sat there with tears streaming down my cheeks while the waitress glared daggers at my then-boyfriend assuming he was crushing my soul." — **An Caillen C.**

"An ex-boyfriend brought me a giant bouquet of flowers at a football game, and 5 minutes later, one of our friends looked at me and said 'He sure is trying to make up for cheating on you, huh?' I didn't know." — **Megan N.**

"My ex 'wrote me a song' in which he mentioned my brown hair ... . Not long after, I found another copy in a drawer of his bedside table. That copy was written for a blonde. In retrospect, I'm a friggin moron." — **Kerri L.**

"I got a Brazilian wax for my hubs - it was a total fucking disaster." — **Alyson H.**

"On one of our first dates, my husband made me sushi from scratch. With romantic music playing in the background, I gagged on the sushi, ran to the bathroom, and spit it in the toilet." — **Kathryn L.**

"He asked if he could pee on me." — **Laura H.**

Laura H. for the win, here, folks. I don't know that it's going to get any worse than that, although we're all curious: DID YOU LET HIM?

ACT 5 - LEVELING UP

Order in the Court(ing)

"Wait." A guy in the audience looks at the woman next to him. "*Five* acts? Aren't there supposed to be, like, four acts *tops,* if he's supposedly writing this in a play format?"

The woman blinks at him. "Have you never read anything of his?" she answers. "The man can barely use correct punctuation, never mind piece together something cohesive. In fact, he's probably writing this very conversation to explain why this format makes zero sense."[1]

somewhere out there, Rodney hits "Save" on his word processor

house lights dim and the curtains open

The stage appears to be set inside a courtroom. Two tables are in the foreground, and a large judge's bench is against the back wall. The judge's chair is empty, but beside the bench is the witness box where we find our protagonist sitting with a terrified look on his face, sweating profusely. This will be the actor's first time doing a monologue, and he's pretty much shitting his pants right now.

Bailiff: Please rise for the honorable Judge Bon Jovi.

The back door opens, and no shit, Jon Bon Jovi enters the courtroom in a judge's robe. The auditorium goes nuts because these tickets were less than $5, and there were no hints there would be a surprise guest.

14 pairs of panties land on the stage followed by two pair of visibly shart-stained tighty-whiteys

---

[1] Editor's Note: This woman does indeed know Rodney very well. By now in the raw draft of the book, I'm ready to develop cat allergies so I have a reason to stop editing. So many adverbs to kill and bad punctuation and sentence structure to fix ... you people don't know how good you have it. *makes note to explain passive voice to Rod before next book*

> **Judge Bon Jovi:** Thank you. Let's proceed with the case of *State vs. Lame Boyfriend.*

He bangs the gavel against the desk and sits down. Three bras and an oxygen mask hit the stage. In row two, an elderly woman gasps for breath but feels it's totally worth it if it scores her a backstage pass.

A smartly dressed man—obviously a lawyer for the prosecution because he looks like a smug jackass—walks out from behind one of the tables. He addresses the crowd and a fake jury made from a leftover backdrop of a *Damn Yankees* production.

> **Jackass Prosecutor:** The State intends to prove, your honor, that the defendant, Mr. Lame Boyfriend, is solely responsible for the disappearance of his long-term relationship.
>
> **Defense Attorney:** I OBJECT! This is all circumcision evidence!
>
> **Judge Bon Jovi:** Don't you mean, "circumstantial evidence?"
>
> **Defense Attorney:** Sure. (pause) Let's go with that.
>
> **Judge Bon Jovi:** Overruled—*he turns slowly and looks at the defendant*—So, you're being accused of giving love a bad name?

The audience erupts in cheers. Jon winks back at the crowd, smiles, does a finger gun shot, and pretends to blow it out.

The prosecution continues their examination of the witness.

> **Jackass Prosecutor:** Do you deny, Mr. Boyfriend, that over time you simply took your entire relationship for granted?
>
> **Defense Attorney:** I OBJECT! The prosecution is being a honey badger!
>
> **Judge Bon Jovi:** Seriously. You mean "badgering the witness?"
>
> **Defense Attorney:** Honey badger don't give a shit.
>
> **Judge Bon Jovi:** Overruled AGAIN.

The defendant fidgets in his chair. He leans forward and a bead of sweat drips from his nose. Jon Bon Jovi whispers, "Gross," because it's a little-known fact that he hates perspiration when it lands on oak surfaces, providing inspiration for the song "Social Disease."[1]

Mr. Lame Boyfriend: Well, there was a time when the relationship was really strong. We did crazy, spontaneous things for each other and weren't afraid of displaying our affection in public.

Judge Bon Jovi: Did you lay your hands on her, or lie her down on a bed of roses?

audience continues to go nuts for these references, but it appears that the elderly lady has either passed out or died

Mr. Lame Boyfriend: Of course, but I never gave her BAD MEDICINE.

crickets

Jackass Prosecutor: So why did you stop tending to the relationship?

Defense Attorney: I object, your honor, on the grounds that this is all speculum.

Judge Bon Jovi: SPECULATION. A speculum is a tool used by gynecologists.

a woman yells "WOO" from the audience and everyone becomes uncomfortable for a minute

Judge Bon Jovi: Overruled. Seriously, did you even go to law school?

Defense lawyer opens wallet, glances at his University of Phoenix Law School wallet-sized laminate of his diploma and sits down

Mr. Lame Boyfriend: I guess I just took her for granted. I always assumed that she knew how I felt, so I didn't bother with the little daily things to remind her.

Judge Bon Jovi: I bet that felt like she was shot through the heart. You

---

[1] Strictly my hypothesis, although I dreamed about this one night after washing down a Vicodin with NyQuil, and it was pretty realistic.

almost can't blame her for being a runaway.

He stands up and fist-pumps, and seriously, no one can blame him because these are amazing references. He's totally killing it.

Mr. Lame Boyfriend: I guess so. In the beginning I did so much just to win her over, and then, once I did, everything went on cruise control. I guess you could say I was livin' on a prayer.

more crickets

Mr. Lame Boyfriend: Sonofabitch.

The judge sits back down, and grabs his gavel.

Judge Bon Jovi: I've heard enough. I hereby find the defendant gui—

Bailiff: WAIT!

The judge stops mid-swing of his hammer. Everyone turns to look at the court officer as he slowly and deliberately moves to the middle of the stage. There, he peels off a mustache and removes a gray wig, revealing a luscious head of long, dark brown hair. Everyone gasps as they realize that the bailiff is actually a beautiful woman.

Defense Attorney: OLD MAN JENKINS!

Judge Bon Jovi takes this opportunity to throw the gavel at the idiot lawyer, striking him in the forehead and knocking him out. Applause erupts and more clothing hits the stage, making it painfully obvious that over 90% of the theater is now naked. In the control booth, the auditorium manager is calculating how much it's going to cost to steam-clean everything and begins drinking from a flask he pulled from his coat.

The female bailiff walks up to the defendant.

Female Bailiff: I heard everything you said. I want to give us another chance if you promise me you won't take our relationship for granted ever again. Also, you're sweating a lot and it's really igging me out.

Judge Bon Jovi: I hear that.

Mr. Lame Boyfriend: I promise to show you every day how much you mean to me. In these arms, I'm all about lovin' you. Just, never say goodbye.

the audience cheers

Judge Bon Jovi: Well played, and remember, keep the faith.

Mr. Lame Boyfriend: Okay. I think we've had enough of that.

Bon Jovi bangs the gavel on the bench, shouts, "Case dismissed!" and stage-dives into the audience. Reaching the second row, he places the previously discarded oxygen mask back on the elderly lady's face. As she regains consciousness, he scoops her up and places her atop a steel horse that's a leftover prop from the musical production of *Troy*.

Elderly Lady: Ride, cowboy, ride!

"Wild in the Streets" blasts over the sound system as they pass the newly reconciled bailiff and her boyfriend. It's a little confusing because the song doesn't make sense as a closing number, but no one complains, because seriously, the tickets were just $5.

I. What's Happenin', Hot Stuff?

If you didn't get the gist from the opening scene, this particular section is about things you *can* do, *should* do, or *shouldn't* do to keep your relationship fresh, and also how to kick it up a notch. One way I've heard to keep a relationship fresh is to douche or give yourself an enema. I may be confusing "keeping things fresh" with "getting ready to make an adult film."

Maybe I should have said these are things to keep your bond interesting. Now it sounds like I'm talking about glue. Did you know there's such a thing as a glue fetish? I should stop while I'm ahead.

> "Guys: If you haven't told your woman she's beautiful today, WTF ARE YOU WAITING FOR?!?!" — **Rodney Lacroix Tweet, December 2014**

Yes. Sometimes my favorite quotes are the ones I say myself. It probably won't surprise you to learn I've endorsed myself for "narcissism" on LinkedIn.

That Tweet up there is part of my mantra. Very early on in my relationship with my wife, I told her not a single day would go by without me saying how beautiful she was. In hindsight, this wasn't a good idea because she has a calendar she only uses to mark the days I *don't* say it and holds it against me at Christmas.

She can be vicious.

However, there are a lot more unmarked boxes on that calendar than marked ones. In my defense, my wife is very hot, so telling her how pretty she is comes easily. Having the forethought to add "tell wife she is beautiful" into my Outlook calendar as a daily recurring appointment (with a reminder that pops up on my phone) also helps a lot, because I'm old and forget things.

If you find it difficult to tell the object of your affection that he/she is attractive, you may have other issues, or the person may, in fact, be ugly. A rule of thumb is if the only picture they've ever given you of themselves is a Glamour Shot, even they think they're not very good looking. Right now some guy is reading this, picturing his desk at work with the three fuzzy Glamour Shot portraits of his wife and thinking, "OH MY GOD."

My guess is if you're pursuing—or in—a relationship with someone, it's because YOU find them attractive, and really, that's all that matters. Unless they're ugly, but like, super rich. Then just suck it up for the greater good of owning really cool gadgets.

There are several key areas you can compliment someone on that will not only endear you to them, but will also make them more confident in themselves and your relationship. If you're great at bullshitting people, this section should be easy for you.

For the Guys

Guys, I know our first instinct is to go for easy flattery, but telling a woman she has a "nice rack" isn't what I'm talking about. That is, unless you're married or in a committed relationship, and you're heading out on the town, AND she's pushing those babies out with a $200 Victoria's Secret bra.

This is especially true if her boobs look like quarter-filled water balloons or flapjacks with stretch-mark syrup because she'll know you're lying immediately, and then, sir, you are screwed and will have to go through three weeks of "ARE YOU HAVING AN AFFAIR?" interrogations.

Here is a short list of things women enjoy being complimented on:
- Almost everything.

Here is a short list of things women *don't* enjoy being complimented on:
- Unusually large zits.
- Unibrow/Mustache/Stray hairs, in general.

- How veiny their boobs are.
- Grey or white hair.
- The cavernous depth of their wrinkles.

Tell her you get lost in her eyes.

You: MY GOD! I'M LOST IN YOUR EYES! LET ME OUT! IT'S DARK AND SCARY IN HERE!

Her: What?

Not like that.

Tell her you love her face. Just remember, guys, make sure she knows she is beautiful to you in some way every single day and you won't have to worry about her nailing the UPS guy unless he bought this book before you did. If that's the case, you may still have time because he's working his way through the neighborhood wives, and he's only up to the Miller's house right now.

For the Ladies

Yes. Even men enjoy getting a compliment every so often because it helps our self-esteem. PLEASE TREAD CAREFULLY, though, because overdoing it may result in your man being so confident in his looks/abilities that he'll start fishing for them regularly.

I know this because my wife once told me I nailed an Eric Cartman impression, and now I answer every one of her questions with, "I'M JUST BIG BONED," trying to get that mojo back.

My wife cries sometimes.

Here is a list of things you can freely tell your man to make him feel good and wanted without him thinking you're lying or fishing for free jewelry.

- You look good in (that shirt/those jeans/me).
- I love your butt. (This is a favorite of mine because I like when my wife tells me I have a cute butt. In reality, I do have a cute butt so that helps and is super-believable.)

- I like how you drive a car.

And now, a short list of things you *shouldn't* compliment men on:
- How fast they finish, thus allowing you to get back to watching Grey's Anatomy.

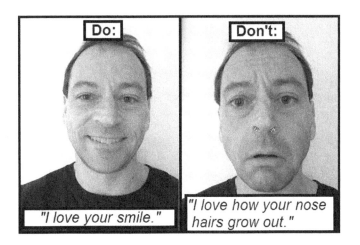

Guys like to feel virile. "Virile" is a weird name for a stripper and we usually get thrown out of the place for trying to feel her, but whatever.

In fact, as a ridiculous coincidence, Kerri sent me this instant message as I was writing this very page:

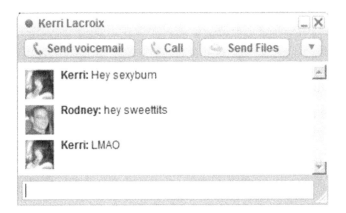

See? She knows how to start a conversation.

I told you I had a cute butt, didn't I?

II. Roses Are Red, and So Is Blood

Search the Internet for "romantic ideas," and you'll come across pictures like this:

No, those are not skin tags. Since this is a black-and-white picture, I will clarify. This is the old "rose petals on the bed" chestnut.

I cannot stress enough how much you SHOULD NOT DO THIS.

You see, once upon a time I had the idea, prior to my woman's arrival, of doing this very thing.

I will line the floors and bed with rose petals, and she will gasp and be smitten, and damn I'm good, I thought.

has drink in my own honor

So I went to my local flower shop and bought a bag of rose petals. The bag set me back $60, and I really wish that was a typo because, seriously, $60?! I may open my own flower shop that just sells flower petals. I'll call it "Petal Pushers" and become instantly rich.

At the time, I was living in an apartment that had wall-to-wall carpeting and was directly over an old deaf guy who liked to watch porn. I'm not sure why I need to mention that, other than to inform you that listening to full-blast porn through your floor is not nearly as awesome as it seems. It also tends to keep you awake most nights. This book is like an encyclopedia of crap you really don't need to know.

I entered my apartment and began spreading the rose petals along the floor, making a path to the bedroom (oh yeah, baby) where I scattered the petals all over my bedspread. Then I put out some candles, shaved my junk[1], and got ready for the visit and the ridiculous amount of loving that would surely ensue.

And ensue it did. The reaction I got was exactly what I was looking for. Her face was a combination of surprise, shock, and adoration. It was amazing even though I mainly only saw the top of her head.

holds hand up for high-five

The next day I awoke and began cleaning up the scattered rose petals. As I picked each petal off my tan bedspread, I noticed an exact replica of the petal was still sitting there. Somehow, in the middle of the night, I had perfected cloning.

I wish.

The replica of the rose petal was in the form of a big, red, stain.

Oh no.

There had to be 400 of those damn petals in that bag. I quickly brushed all of the petals from the bedspread and was faced with what appeared to be a mattress covered in severe acne. WHAT THE HELL. Thinking quickly, I spritzed some ProActiv on it but the rose zits stayed put. I ran to the kitchen for some cleaner, but I was a bachelor at the time, so the only thing under my

---

[1] That is an embedded extra tip, right there: shave your junk if you're planning on a night of romance. Nothing ruins the mood like a guy continually picking something out of his front teeth or a woman trying to cough up a hairball for three minutes.

sink was a wire scouring pad from 1976.

I looked at the bag the petals came in. There was no "Hey idiot, these things make stains" warning or "Do not put on surfaces that are lighter than black in color" hint to suggest this would happen. I knelt down and slowly peeled a rose petal off my beige carpet.

Carpet zit.

YOU'VE GOT TO BE KIDDING ME.

Under every single rose petal was an identical red stain. Every single one. On my bed. On the floor. On the carpet. Even the one I peeled off my left ass cheek left a stain, but that one was cute because it was a little heart-shaped one.

My attempts at cleaning both the bedspread and carpet were fruitless. In the end, I had a professional carpet cleaner come in, and I bought new linens. Between the flowers and the damage they caused, my total for a night of romance was in the ballpark of $400.

I can tell you, men, no matter what she lets you do to her, $400 is not worth it.

Sorry, $600.

You see, I also didn't get half of my security deposit back after moving out, due to what management called "Cost to clean blood stains in bedroom carpeting." Apparently, in my mad dash to clear my bed of the stain-petals, a bunch flew under the bed where they went on to bleed into my carpet and subsequently drain my checking account.

It's like the song goes:

"Every Rose Has Its Thorn" but by "thorn" they mean "stuff that ruins bedspreads and carpet."

III. Wanna Get Away? Not Really, No.

Every couple thinks of having a nice, quiet, romantic interlude away from their hectic life. They look at planning a cruise or staying at a nice bed-and-breakfast. Maybe it's for a week, a weekend, or in the case of parents, 20 minutes of peace and goddamn quiet without being asked to help open a juice box.

I have two kids and two step-children, which is why I spend so much time in my soundproofed bathroom pretending to shit.

If you have the time and wherewithal (OMG I can't believe I spelled that right on the first try), then I have some suggestions on where NOT to go, based on my own experiences. I'm not saying you can't go there, I'm saying that if you go to these locations, do the opposite of what I did.

Getaway to Avoid #1: The Romantic Camping Trip

First off, the words "romantic" and "camping trip" do not belong in the same sentence. There is absolutely nothing romantic about camping unless you're in a tent that you smuggled inside your luggage while staying at the Ritz Carlton.

My very first "getaway" with a woman was a camping trip on a 4th of July weekend. I don't know whose idea it was, but I'm going to assume it was hers because I hate the outdoors, so yes, let's blame her.

Within five minutes of our arrival at the site and attempting to put up the tent, (a) we were arguing, (b) I was being punched, and (c) somehow, she had taken off my shoes during my beating and was throwing them at my head.

Nothing says "romantic getaway" like being hit in the temple with a Nike traveling 25 miles per hour while you're trying to bang tent stakes into the ground using a can of beef stew.

That's when the rain started.

Of course, the rain brought mosquitos and since mosquitos bring malaria we opted for bug spray. I can sincerely tell you that—after dodging airborne sneakers—nothing quells the desire in a man's loins quite like the smell of bug spray and the bitter, slightly poisonous taste of DEET.

I was a bit too late on the bug spray as a mosquito had managed to sting my eyelid. I looked like a shiny, smelly welterweight boxer.

"Should we just go home?" I asked.

She looked at me, still grasping one of my sneakers. "We just got here."

Of course, no camping trip is complete without a trip to the restrooms. A great test for men who think they're in love is to stand guard over a rocket-shaped outhouse as their girlfriend is inside near-puking while trying to take a dump.

And while you're listening to this horror, you're picturing her turd landing on someone else's turd like a really gross reverse-version of *Jenga*.

We decided to stick it out, and the rest of the weekend was downhill from there. On the bright side, I was able to cross "poop on top of someone else's poop while sitting in a fake rocket ship" off of my bucket list.

Yes, my bucket list is terrible.

Suffice it to say our campsite neighbors had plenty of entertainment. I'm almost positive I could hear them laughing when my girlfriend threw my parachute pants in the fire after I told her to stop complaining about the noise our inflatable mattress was making.

That pitched tent inside the Ritz Carlton sounds so much better, doesn't it?

IV. The Shocker

I call this one "The Shocker" because (a) I'm nothing if not inappropriate and love creating innuendo and (b) see "a."

Actually, this chapter is about sending her a love note. I titled it "The Shocker," though, because the trick to sending a truly effective letter of affection is in the surprise. If someone sees or knows something is coming (i.e., the "flowers on Valentine's Day" or when you're making "the face" during nookie) it becomes routine and expected.

Routine is the antichrist of romance. That is a terrible analogy but I'm sticking with it because I can't come up with another one right now, and I think it will sell well on a t-shirt.

Shock value is a major component of being perceived as a hopeless romantic. This does not mean you tear open the shower curtain on your wife while holding a running chainsaw with "I lurve yoo" written in fake blood on it—although OHMYGOD that is a great idea. See drawing.

What I mean by the "element of surprise" is doing something thoughtful that takes very little effort and interrupts a normally monotonous day.

Example #1:

I live in Southern New Hampshire where the summer temps range from hot to stifling, and the winter temps can be anywhere between "Holy shit it's wicked cold" and "Jesus, it's wicked fucking cold."

This means that during the winter, our cars are typically covered in giant sheets of ice or snow, requiring them to be cleared off and warmed up on cold mornings. During the months of January and February, paleontologists descend upon New England because it is not uncommon to discover wooly mammoth remains or John Leguizamo trapped beneath your windshield wipers.

My wife happens to leave for her hour-long commute to work before I do, so one morning I went out to warm up her car for her (which can, in and of itself, be considered one of the acts of chivalry noted in a previous chapter). As I went to start it, I noticed that all the windows had ice on them so I took it upon myself to write her a note, completely disregarding the pain and suffering caused by scraping my finely manicured nails against cold, bumpy stuff: I <3 U

Now before you say, "I can't believe he took a picture of this" and "I bet he did this just for the book," I should tell you that even though that would have been an amazing idea, I'm not that smart.

When my wife left for work and found my impromptu note, she's the one who took the picture and posted it on her Facebook wall with *"Awwww ... I love you too baby."*

Then she tagged me in the photo.

Of course I replied, "WHO WROTE THIS TO YOU? I WILL KILL HIM," because I'm a dick like that.

Her posting this means that both her friends *and* my friends saw it. This also means that all my guy friends hated me just a little bit more that morning because I'm good at making them look like insensitive jerkfaces.

But this is the stuff I'm talking about. It took zero effort or time to do but made an impact on the woman I love. It also made an impact on my fingernails, but if I gripe about them here I'll sound like a real pussy.

Ladies, your version of this would be to use lipstick to write a message on the bathroom mirror if you happen to leave before him. Do not do this if your guy is a freak about cleaning the house, like I am. Even though you wrote, *"You're everything to me"* on the mirror, I'm thinking *"What the hell am I going to use to wipe this crap off without it streaking?"*

As a child, my mom instilled a desire in me to keep things clean and orderly. It's been ruining my love of spontaneity ever since. Thanks a lot, Mom. Also, call me after you read this because I need to know how to get lipstick off the mirror.

Example #2:

Both the wife and I brown-bag our lunches because between the two of us, we have four kids, and unless you're Stephen King, being an author isn't all that lucrative. I hope this book changes that. Make sure your friends buy their own copies instead of borrowing yours. That should help with my money situation. Thanks in advance.

Regardless, we each usually make our own lunches, but one morning my wife asked me to make hers. Of course this required me to ask 68 questions about how many slices of cheese and what condiments and how many pickles do you wa—what? No pickles?

Great, I married an insane woman. Who doesn't put pickles on their sandwich? OKAY FINE NO PICKLES. Jesus. But seriously, how do you eat a sandwich without pickles? That's so stupid. Stupid and sad. I'm getting angry just thinking about it.

I crafted her pickle-less pitiful excuse for a "sandwich" and started wrapping it in foil. The top slice of the sandwich bread stared at me, blankly.

"Why no pickles?" it asked. As a single tear rolled down my cheek, I couldn't give an answer, but staring at that bland piece of bread gave me a great idea.

And so later that day, I received yet another Facebook notification that I had been tagged in a photo on my wife's wall:

Her description of the photo was simply, "Awwww."

This was followed by all her female friends commenting, "You have a sweet husband," and "MY husband doesn't do this," with all the guys writing, "OMG why is he such an asshole?"

Yes, I'm an asshole, but I'm a romantic asshole. A romantic asshole who turned the mundane act of opening a sandwich into a wonderful surprise for my woman.

Sorry. "Sandwich" should be in quotes there. Having no pickles disqualifies it.

She's lucky I love her, or this would be so over.

V: 43 Shades of Aquamarine

When it comes to romance, I'm always trying to outdo myself. I'm also always trying to do myself, which is why I'm at the orthopedist a lot and have double sessions with my therapist.

You may be surprised to know that injuries sustained while trying to stretch your wiggly to your bung are not covered by most health insurance plans so check with your carrier.

thumbs through list of maladies covered by Obamacare just to see

On the very first Christmas Kerri and I shared together, I gave her the best present last, as is my usual custom. Always giving someone the big-ticket or thoughtful item last helps them to forget that you also got them deodorant and breath mints as stocking stuffers.

She opened the wrapping and stared down at the amazing gift I had given her.

Her: Cute.

Then she thumbed through it, said "cute" again, and put it down.

I was dumbfounded.

This was her big gift. This book.

This was her thoughtful present. The gift that everything I had given her prior, including the Powder Fresh Secret and 4 packs of

Mentos, had led up to. This was the crescendo of my Christmas gift concert, and all I got was a half-hearted "cute," a few flipped pages, and she put it down?

I was crushed. CRUSHED. This was the Sofia Vergara nowhere-within-fifty-feet court order fiasco happening all over again.

That's when she looked down at the cover and saw the words: *"by Rodney"*

She picked the book up again and opened the pages. She stopped. Her mouth dropped open, and she looked at me.

Kerri: Wait. Did you make this yourself?

Me: I did.

peacock tail opens wide behind my ass

And that's when I saw the tear come to her eye as she turned a few more pages. The tear rolled down her cheek and she did that thing she always does when I happen to hit the home run and floor her with something unexpected ...

Kerri: OH, HONEEEEY!

Inside my head I was doing a gigantic happy dance that included the Sprinkler and a spot-on version of the Robot. I was so relieved she didn't blow off everything I had just worked on, because honestly, that would have sucked lots of donkey balls.

Speaking of donkey balls, have you ever wondered how that all worked in *Shrek?* The donkey and the dragon have babies, so they must have boinked, right? Someone needs to make an animation of that—maybe "hidden camera footage" style.

checks NetFlix, still nothing

Kerri began flipping through the book with more zeal. After each page she'd give me the pouty lip, and I knew, right then, I was going to get banged so hard that night.

Her response confirmed that my gift was pretty awesome, and it was. Feel free to look up the sites where you can make these gifts on your own. I'm not going to mention them by name here because I have no royalty deal with them. Sucks so badly.

flip

laugh

flip

pouty stare

boing (that one's me)

Every picture flip evoked a different reaction. This one got me a laugh:

Because nothing says "Here's how much I love you" like a picture of a couple about to pass out from alcohol poisoning. I think maybe we should consider going to support meetings because we both looked at each other and said, "SO TRUE!"

About the Author

Rodney Lacroix is typically a self-centered know-it-all with narcissistic tendencies. He thinks he's funny and thinks you should think he's funny, too (see narcissistic comment).

Rodney usually only thinks of himself, except when it comes to his kids..

..and his girlfriend, Kerri.

Of course I started the book with an "About the Author" page because I'm nothing if not self-indulgent. This certainly wasn't a surprise to Kerri, plus it made the book a little thicker and funnier, and I'm also all about thick and funny. I don't remember where I was going with that.

flip

She reached the "About the Couple" page and gave me that sweet, pouty look again. As I'm looking at this page now, I realize that it actually looks like she's grabbing my lower spine, so maybe she's a chiropractor here? Or a predator about to rip out my entire skeletal system? The mysteries lying herein are turning this into a shitty knockoff of *The Da Vinci Code*.

knocks on wood this book makes 1/1000000th the profit of that one

In hindsight I should have put hair on Kerri's head but I did this at work, and there's only so much time I can goof around

About the Couple

The story of Kerri and Rodney began with two memberships on Match.com, some amazing profile editing and - of course - the incomparable Susan Boyle.

Some instant messages and phone calls later the two worked their sexytime magic and thus helped create what some would later call "the hottest couple of all time outside Brangelina."

before getting caught. I'm actually on my 7th year of slacking off at work, so I think my days are numbered.

flip

Kerri was one of the three people in the world who owned a BlackBerry phone at the time. She would CONSTANTLY text on the thing while she was driving. Sometimes with me in the car, staring on in horror. Typically, she would be texting me as I sat two feet away in the passenger seat.

This is because she knows what starting a verbal conversation with me can lead to, and she's had far too many of those that ended up in discussions about donkey-dragon sex.

She also had an issue with her keyboard stutter tttttyyyypppping characters, which is why I mentioned it in the book.

She now uses an iPhone and has to deal with terrible autocorrect suggestions like when she wanted me to buy Triscuits at the store but typed "True its," and long story short, I was in that goddamn store for three hours. Screw you, Apple.

I got a lot of awesome feedback from this gift (read: sex for 20 minutes), so I thought I'd pass this little nugget along to you as well—Fill the book with things that only the two of you know about (like how you cannot read a single text message without having to correct "you're" vs "your" or that they fart in their sleep).

Sounds weird, I know, but pointing out that they fart in their sleep and wake themselves up can turn it into a romantic gesture. Trust me, I know on this one.

It's a page in the book.

VI: Wanna Try Getting Away Again? Nope. Not Even A Little.

If you're still thinking about getting away for a weekend after reading that camping story a few chapters back, I hope you've at least decided to make better choices on where to go. With that segue, I present to you another romantic vacation story gone south. Enjoy.

Getaway to Avoid #2: Rubbing Me the Wrong Way

"I love a massage. I'd go every day if I could. I don't need to be wrapped in herbs like a salmon fillet, but I do love a massage." — **Jason Bateman**

Jason Bateman and I do not have that one thing in common. Let me explain.

While on a weekend getaway in the New Hampshire mountains, Kerri and I booked a "couples massage" at a spa. Unfortunately, the hotel we stayed at also had an indoor water park.

Yes, an indoor water park sounds pretty awesome, if you're six years old. At our age, though, sharing a bath with thousands of kids doesn't sound like fun.

This sentiment was not shared by the rest of the hotel vacationers: families who planned their stay around said indoor water park. This meant we were two adults trying to enjoy a kid-free weekend while being completely surrounded by 36,000 screaming children in bathing suits.

As an added bonus, all of these children sounded like they were jumping on the floor directly above our room.

In an attempt to have some romantic, non-screaming adult time on our vacation, we booked a couples massage at the hotel's spa. I had no idea what to expect because I'd never had any type of massage, unless you count having a herniated disc operated on as a rubdown.

Correction: a herniated disc that looked like an insect when I saw the MRI.

Freaky, right? I KNOW.

We were told to strip down to whatever we felt comfortable in, slip under the towels on our respective tables, and wait for the massage therapists to join us. So we did, and my beautiful woman and I lay six feet apart from each other, alone in the room together, each naked except for a plush towel. And that's when it happened.

Me: Ummmm ...

Kerri: What?

Me: Boing.

Kerri: Boing?

I wiggled my eyebrows at her.

Her eyes opened wide and I could tell she knew the answer before she even said it.

Kerri: OH NO YOU DON'T HAVE A BONER.

I did. I did have a boner. It was a very unfortunate boner because even though the table has a hole to put your face into, it does not have a hole to put your erection through. This seems like a serious design flaw.

And not only that, the erection was pointed down toward my feet and squished up against the table. I was about to adjust myself to make it a little more "north-facing" when the door to the room opened, and the two massage therapists entered.

The first therapist was beautiful. Black polo shirt, long brown hair, and a gorgeous smile. She looked at me and said, "Hi," before sidling up next to Kerri's table.

Damn.

Then Helga walked in.

Helga was 250 pounds of sheer muscle and had the body of an Olympic power lifter. Giant sausages posed as fingers at the ends of her thick, hairy arms, and her hair was pulled back so tight her eyes bulged.

"ARGLEBARGLE!" she said in the tongue of her native mutant-land place.

I really don't know what she said because I wasn't paying attention. I was watching the *hot* therapist oil up the back of—

Me (thinking): *Oh. Oh man. I'm really going to need to adjust this penis. It's starting to hurt, and now that I'm watching some hot girl-on-girl action just an arm's length away, it's getting quite worse.*

I made a quick attempt to raise my ass off the bench, which would have automatically righted my stiffy. However, as I began to lift my butt, Helga's meaty mitts pushed down on my lower lumbar, crunching my little Rodney head-first into the bench.

Me: UNGHH.

Helga: I haven't even started.

Helga reached into the nearby fishbowl and swallowed a frog whole.

To my right, I heard a stifled giggle. I looked over to see the rubdown continuing on the next table. Oil everywhere, hot therapist kneading and pressing and—

Me: OHMYGODSONOFABITCH.

Helga: Was that too hard?

I'll show you something too hard, I thought.

Me: A little, yeah.

It felt like being walked on by an army of Stormtroopers. Who the hell enjoys this?!

Out of the corner of my eye, I could see my therapist reaching back to her side table to get more oil. *This is my moment to right myself*, I thought. *I must be quick.*

I raised my buttocks upward to allow a penile relocation, but Helga had already returned. She firmly pressed down on my back.

prrrrrrrrrpppppppppttttttttttt

The fart squeezed out quickly, loudly, and with a tinge of sharpness. I don't know if you've ever had a sharp fart, but it feels like you toot out a rusty nail. It happened so fast I barely had time to clench my ass, so the very end transformed into a soprano-like high note.

prrrrrrrpppppppptttttttttt-fwwweeeeeeeeee

Oh. My. God.

That solved the boner problem because all the blood in my body rushed to my face. I'd just *farted away a boner* in a room full of women, two of them very attractive.

Helga was stone-faced and professional. She prepared to go in for another round of punishment.

Helga: Happens all the time. Don't worry about it.

Me: I'm done.

Helga: But I haven't even star—

Me: DONE.

Helga backed away from the table as my dignity wafted around the room. I was a bit woozy as I sat up, but I clutched my towel around me and teetered off the table. Kerri was dying laughing, and the hot therapist barely held back her own laughter.

So much for a romantic couples massage.

I grabbed my clothes and opened the door, then hesitated and turned to Kerri.

Me: If you need me, I'll be at the water park.

VII: Hey, That's a Nice Box

Her: THIS IS ONE OF THE GREATEST GIFTS OF ALL TIME.

Yes. My wife called it one of the greatest romantic gifts OF ALL TIME. I have to agree with this assessment, saying that as someone who got a whole lotta love after giving it.

Thankfully I'm not talking about the Led Zeppelin kind, because they're an overrated band (a lot of middle-aged people who still smoke pot on the regular don't like me right now).

But let's start at the beginning ...

She unwrapped the present, peeling off the "It's a Boy!" paper with a quizzical look on her face. I will wrap gifts with anything I can find. I once wrapped a wedding present in black paper with a Grim Reaper caricature on it, because it's all I had after getting my friend something for his 40th birthday party. The bride was not amused.

She reached in and pulled out a large, pink box. You have no idea how difficult it is for me to not write some sort of sexual joke right here. And now that I've spelled it out, you probably do have an idea. I think this is called "innuendo."

adds "English Scholar" to resume

My wife untied the pink ribbon and opened the lid, and amidst a sea of black tissue paper (seriously, I think I overbought for that wedding gift), were a bunch of tiny envelopes.

Each envelope had a word written on it, like so:

Her: You couldn't find anything other than black tissue paper?

Ugh. My wrapping choices always come back to haunt me. She pulled out one of the envelopes.

Her: What is it?

Me: It's an elephant.

Sometimes I can be a jerk.

Me: Just open one.

She opened the envelope, mouthed what was written on the card inside, and started crying.

TIP: If you can give your girl something that makes her cry, and it doesn't involve twisting her nipple really, really hard, then you've done well.

The envelope contained a love note. Looking up, she realized she now had a box full of them. Each note was different and painstakingly handcrafted. I say "painstakingly" because my wrist cramped up, twice.

A few days earlier, I had been scrambling for the perfect birthday gift. I was literally blowing my proverbial romantic load by upping the ante at every occasion. I'd backed myself into my own gift-giving corner.

That's about when I walked into a dollar store and found these:

Perfect.

I grabbed 41 of the cards and envelopes because it would be her 41st birthday, and—based on my scientific calculations—that seemed like the right amount for what I was going to do.

Then I grabbed a bunch of extra ones because I almost always misspell something when I'm filling things out. This usually happens when I'm refinancing my mortgage and have to sign my name 600 times. By the halfway point, I'm autographing documents as "Ringlefork W. Lipidkoi."

While I was at it, I grabbed some beef jerky because you can't beat $1 for beef jerky. I love the dollar store.

And to make my visit even more fun, I always put on a fake European accent and ask the employees, "HOW MUCH DIS?" while holding the items high over my head.

You should try it. It's fun making them say, "a dollar," over and over again in increasingly agitated tones.

If you decide to do the "love note card" thing but can't find cards at a dollar store, you can find them at a typical Hallmark-type store. They'll be in the stationery section where they sell envelopes and gift bags and crap like that.

Remember to go past the cute wooden signs that say "I Love You More," "Because Nana Says So," and "It's Wine O'Clock," and go directly to the stationery section. Stay strong, my friend.

Also, be prepared to shell out more money, and maybe walk out with a Precious Moments impulse-buy that'll sit in one of your house corners collecting dust for decades.

The more you know.

rainbow star goes by

The original picture I inserted on the previous page is vibrantly colored, but it costs extra to print in color which cuts into my profit margin, so you'll just have to use your creativity. Imagine cards and envelopes in brilliant pinks and reds and purples, and maybe a nude celebrity of your choosing. I don't care.

Whatever you do, don't get grey or dark grey cards like the picture shows. You're trying to be romantic, not show off your Ph.D. in Accounting.

I had to have a fancy box to put the cards in. And since this was a special event, I passed on my first knee-jerk thought of dumping them in a shoebox.

Whenever I need to put something in a box[1], I immediately run to the basement where there's always a plethora of shoe boxes. I'm not sure why this is, exactly, but if you're a parent then you have 50 or so lying around because at some point your kid is going to need to build a diorama for school. If the only shoeboxes you have in the house contain clay Snow Leopards, you may have to find another type of box.

---

[1] There are so many jokes writing themselves in this story it's ridiculous.

I felt the need to include a picture of my son's (my) diorama from 3rd grade that he (I) did and on which he (I) got an A+. Why teachers insist on having kids (parents) make dioramas is beyond me, but I think he does (I do) an amazing job on them, and I like keeping stuff like this around to showcase his (my) talent.

> Dear teachers: Stop giving kids projects like this. I graduated years ago just so I wouldn't have to do any more school work. Thank you in advance.

This concludes our sidebar. Now let's get back to the project and the cards.

It took me a while, but I found the perfect box. I've seen all kinds of boxes in my lifetime an—

Sorry. Too easy.

We're about to expand on the "Reasons Why I Love You" idea that was mentioned earlier, so make sure you haven't exhausted your resources. On that note, if you can't find 30 noteworthy things about your significant other, or your relationship in general, then you should use your box to pack up some of your things and move out. Depending on how much stuff you own, you may need a bigger box.

I began my brainstorming by thinking of some categories.

For your information, the purpose of the cards is to give your lover a short one-liner about something you find special about him or her, or even just the relationship in general. My categories included:

- "I ..."
- "We ..."
- "You Are ..."
- "I Love ..."
- "Sometimes ... "

I purposely tried to avoid such categories as:

- "I really hate ..."
- "You suck at ..."
- "I'm so grossed out when ..."
- "WTF is up with ..."

Believe it or not, those cards are an argument waiting to happen.

I realized I bought too many cards, so decided it was safer to use my neighbor's trash to throw the extras away. I didn't want my wife discovering evidence before I gave her the gift.

For added entertainment value, I wrote "*Thanks for last night*" on one of them, crumpled it slightly, and placed atop their recycling bin. Then I made some popcorn and waited for the fireworks when my neighbor's spouse would hopefully find it.

I have way too much time on my hands.

You can also buy additional cards if you run out but still have a ton of stuff to say. That last sentence is more accurate for women, because in general, men are lazy and don't like to think. Plus, we're busy dropping "*Thanks for last night*" cards in random trash bins throughout the neighborhood. Guys are also assholes and entertained by stuff like this.

I began writing my love notes on the cards, deciding it was best to write whatever came to the tip of my tongue. This is why thirteen of the cards said "canker sore," and had to be tossed, causing even greater confusion at my neighbor's house.

Here's an example of one of the cards for my wife:

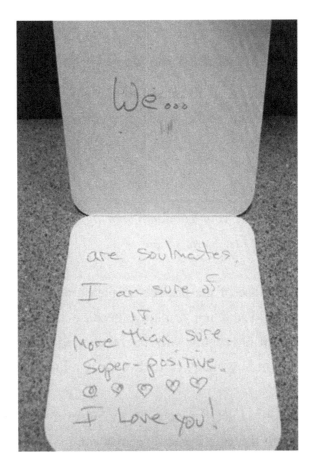

I made an effort to write "I Love You!" at the end of every card just in case she forgot I loved her. Reinforcement never hurts. This is especially true if your loved one has short-term memory loss, or is a guy and doesn't hear what you say the first 200 times you say it.

I numbered all the cards so she could open them chronologically, and placed them in the box. I considered skipping a number here and there so I could watch her empty the whole thing while swearing at me. If you get the inkling to do this, make sure you evaluate your relationship really well before attempting it, because you may wind up a victim of paper-cut manslaughter.

My intention was for her to open one card every week, which would have made this the gift that kept on giving for almost a year. However, after she opened the first card, she decided she didn't want to wait a week to open the next one. That kind of ruined my plans, but she's a woman and that's what women do.

Women: ruining the plans of men since the dawn of time.

IMPORTANT NOTE: A good rule of thumb is to not write the cards for this project when she's kept you up all night snoring, because you don't want her doing this on day #3:

pulls out an "I ..." card

opens card

reads out loud: I ... hate your goddamn snoring because I haven't slept for more than 3 hours in the last 5 years

cries

This defeats the purpose of the project, so please don't do this. Make sure you're in a good mood and not drinking, because if you're loaded, I can guarantee you half of the cards will be misspelled or contain the word "boobies." I can't count how many cards I've thrown into my neighbor's trash because of this.

Since it was *her* gift, I let her open them however she wanted. Letting women get away with things is something men do, mainly because we don't want to hear them complain.

So, she opened one envelope a day for the next 41 days, first thing in the morning, and I got the "aww" look and a hearty smooch after every single one.

Sometimes I even got a bum rub after the smooch. It's the little things, people.

licks fingertip and places on hip ... makes "psssshhh" sound

A woman opening one of these cards is akin to verbal foreplay.

TIP: If you're into BDSM then this isn't the best foreplay idea because it will ruin the "I want to squish your things really hard with these pliers and beat the crap out of you" vibe, unless that's what it says inside one of the cards.

Super Non-funny Sentimental Epilogue

Inside this book you'll find some romantic stories and ideas from my fans. I asked people to give me tales of the most romantic things anyone has done for them. Most are not included in this book specifically because they included stories of vomiting and bowel movements. I don't know why that was, and I stopped asking after reading the sixteenth one. However, I received *this* non-bodily-function-related response from a longtime reader of my blog and fan of my books, Amanda:

> You asked for romantic experiences, so here's the best I have done: My boyfriend (at the time) was about to deploy to Iraq for a year. I bought (and made) 365 cards and notes for him, and gave them to him at the airport preparing to leave. I told him to open one each day.
>
> I spent weeks preparing this for him, and although our relationship didn't end up working out in the long run, he really appreciated the thought, and said it made him feel closer to home every time he opened a new card or letter.

Wow.

It didn't occur to me this project could be used for almost anything, and Amanda's story really floored me. It's a great use for this idea, so some serious kudos to her for doing it and for OHMYGOD having the thoughtfulness, fortitude, and stamina to make a year's worth of cards.

My wrist hurts just thinking about it.

Act 5 Progress Checklist

Are you still awake? Yes, I know, that was a long section.

As an added tip while you read this book, keep saying, "That's what she said," "That's what he said," or "Oh, I get it" after each sentence, like the last one in the above paragraph.

Romantic As Hell: *Providing endless hours of self-serve entertainment.* Let's see how you fared with this section.

	Yes	No
People love getting compliments on features like skin tags and excess mole hairs.	☐	☒
I have a cute butt.	☑	☐
Surprise love notes are the balls.	☑	☐
People who don't like pickles are perfectly normal.	☐	☒
Farting while getting a massage is a fantastic way to express your love.	☐	☒
Making dioramas is fun and exciting.	☐	☒
A book or a box of notes, whatever it is, speaks from the heart.	☑	☐

Entr'acte #3

Lady Chimes

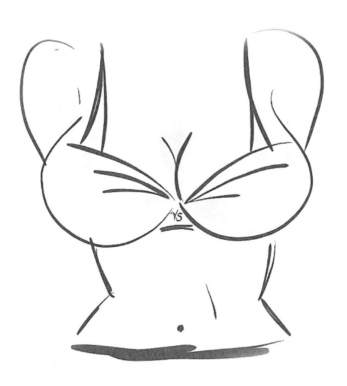

Love Nuggets for the Ladies

Sometimes I read my section titles and think, *That sounds gross*. This is one of those times.

Yes, this book is written by a man, and yes, this book has a lot of info that will help a guy be more romantic, but I am in *no way* forgetting about you beautiful women out there. In fact, I'm thinking of several of you at this very moment.

In my thoughts, you are all together in a sauna and several of you are having pillow fights while wearing only towels. How you got pillows into a steam bath, I have no idea, but let's pretend it involved hair-pulling and maybe some light choking of the busty receptionist.

I've digressed.

Listen, ladies, I know how hard it can be for you to think of romantic things to do for a guy and have him (a) take it seriously, and (b) not be an ass about it. My wife will be the first to tell you that she is terrible at thinking of romantic ideas, and I will be the second person to tell you the same thing. I really hope she skips this section.

EDIT: My wife did not skip this section. She also did not like me saying she wasn't romantic. Here is her actual comment for this page as she was giving me editorial suggestions:

I need to ask her why this angry head has five legs. Is it a centipede? I have no idea. My wife is also terrible at drawing. Also note that this section was originally on page 54, meaning you'd have been done with this book if it was left in its original format. You're probably sad right now.

Since this chapter is written for the ladies, it contains some specific ideas geared toward romancing your man.

Please note that "romancing your man" is a misnomer because a man will never admit to wanting to be romanced. Men are typically too proud or too wrapped up in the weather-woman's busty profile to worry about you wooing them. That's not to say we don't want to be romanced, it's just that—holy cow her boobs are literally covering the entire Eastern Seaboard.

See what I mean? I'm writing you ladies tips and can't even concentrate while this woman is doing the weather. I haven't heard an actual forecast since 1988 because now all I hear when she's doing the weather is "boobs boobs chance of boobs snow boobs."

I asked some of my lady friends about romantic ideas they've done for their guys. I received several responses like "I take my teeth out," "You ain't no cop, are you?" and "Are you gonna pay me, or what?"

Then I got some responses from my lady friends who weren't hookers, and they were a lot less intimidating, and honestly, quite a bit cheaper.

Mix Tapes Aren't Dead

"If you go to concerts, make CDs of the set lists for each show you've gone to over the course of the year. Make the CD cover a picture of the two of you at the show."

This is a great idea unless it's from a Coldplay concert. If that's the case, he's already broken the CD into a billion jillion pieces.

I'm With the Band

"If the guy likes a particular band, make him a basket of collectible items from them. Shirts, drum sticks, guitar picks, etc. You can also get signed band photos if you can find or afford them."

Brilliant. Most guys are pretty passionate about their favorite bands in some way, shape, form, or fashion.

Hopefully this doesn't come in the way, shape, form, or fashion of him dressing up like Gene Simmons, because that's weird, and you should leave him immediately.

He has issues.

I made something similar once (at right). I had some signed guitar picks and a concert ticket mounted inside a display case and given as a gift. Why I give awesome crap like this away instead of

keeping it for myself is a mystery, but I like to think that the recipient's recognition of my self-sacrifice is part of the charm. Personally, if I got something like this as a present it would give me a raging love gun.

Speaking of "love gun," I need to go get my boots on. The KISS concert starts in an hour.

Sure to Score

I'm pretty proud of this project name because this one is about sports so "score" has a double meaning here. As you can see, I impress myself very easily.

Statistics show that nine out of ten men are avid sports fans. The tenth guy is busy making up statistics about how many guys are avid sports fans. So, if your man loves sports, and you love them as well (or at least take in a game or 300 with him to appease his fanaticism), this project gets even better.

Here's the idea:

> *"Make a collage of sports games you've attended together. Include the tickets, box scores and pictures of the two of you at the games."*

That's a pretty cool idea, unless the sport you usually attend is soccer and you happen to live in Europe. I'm not sure that anyone wants to keep a frame full of blood-stained tickets and someone else's teeth that also serves as a constant reminder of the rioting in the stands that left 140 people dead.

There's a reason it's not a popular sport in the United States. We like to keep our sports-related violence in the parking lots and bars after championship victories where it belongs.

This is still a great idea, though, and gets even better if you also have pictures of cheerleaders or maybe the players' wives. Actually, never mind.

That would be distracting, and those photos tend to be hard to get anyway if the court orders and minimum-distance rules against you are still in effect.

I made up a mock-up of one of these showing me and Kerri (the actual event names have been changed to protect the innocent):

As an example.

I think it came out nice (I even left out the cheerleader pictures).

Maybe in addition to a gift like this, you could throw in some playoff tickets for him too. Wouldn't hurt.

You might even get a thank-you gift back. Maybe a nice weekend getaway if the weather is nice. Right now the forecast just calls for "boobs boobies boobs boobs," though.

Act 6 - Do or Do Not Or Maybe Just Run?

I. You Can't Have A "Lifelong Commitment" Without Including the Words "Long Commitment"

I'm going off the beaten path here and not writing this section as though you're watching part of a theater production. I figured you could use a break from it for a little while, and as someone with adult-onset ADD, I totally understand, because steak is my favorite, and I miss the TV show *Cheers*.

We've been ramping up the chronology of this book from the basics into the strong relationship process. Did you enjoy the last *Cheers* episode? I did. I thought it was poetic and—

Sorry.

I figured I'd at least mention the institute of marriage here. It's called "Institute of Marriage" because if you've considered foregoing decades of sex with other people, you should be institutionalized. Um, I love you, Kerri.

ducks

This book isn't how to dupe someone into marrying you, but if that's your thing, you can certainly use the information herein to give it a shot. If it's not your thing, I guess I'll see you on Tinder and maybe we'll hook up sometime? Just saying it's a possibility, and I bring my own lube.

Still love you, Kerri.

dodges crossbow bolts

Venture forth, because here's some advice on taking the leap. Some people who've already taken the leap may be thinking of taking another one right now, probably off a cliff.

Married people are crazy.

Kerri, I really do lo—

is rightfully and deservedly knocked unconscious

II. Why Magic Tricks Should Be Left to David Copperfield

The wedding proposal.

We all think about doing something amazing and special for the person we love when it comes time to make the commitment that tops all other commitments. Of course, I'm talking about sharing a data plan for your cell phones.

Wait. Wedding proposal. I was talking about a wedding proposal.

Women dream about when and how it's going to happen from the time they're little girls.

Men dream about a lifetime of paying off a ring and whether or not she'll give it back if he dumps her? What if she dumps him? If he keeps the receipt, does that show her a lack of sincerity, and she won't fully trust the bond of their relationship? Maybe he'll keep the receipt, but just hide it way in the back of his sock drawer.

So many decisions to consider when proposing marriage, none of them all that good.

Even so, I had made up my mind to ask my girlfriend to marry me. It seemed the next logical step in the relationship since we'd already stopped enjoying spending time with each other.

With no money to have the question appear on the Red Sox Jumbotron where she could say "no" in front of 35,000 people and have hot dogs thrown at her, I began to think ...

Fancy dinner? Maybe.

Hot air balloon ride? Screw that unless she doesn't mind my vomit all over her new ring.

Flash mobs hadn't been invented yet, so that was out, too.

Then I saw a special on television that gave me an idea: magic.

MAGIC?!

YES. I could somehow work my marriage proposal into a magic trick!

What's funny is that even as I write this I can hear you all moaning with disapproval. I can see you reading this as though a train is coming down the proverbial track. I have my back to it, and you're waving your hands, yelling "GET OUT OF THE WAY THERE'S A TRAIN COMING," but I'm thinking, *What? OH MY GOD I'VE GOT THIS MAGIC TRI—*

splat

Thank you for putting me out of my misery, train.

The Night

The diamond ring was a tiny little number that, if you looked at it in just the right light, looked like a very sparkly piece of sand. I stashed it in my pocket and took my girlfriend to our favorite restaurant. I don't even remember the name of the place, but I do recall the floors were knotty pine and the napkins were folded white linens.

I remember this because ...

I looked at my girlfriend during a moment of silence. We had been dating for seven years, so our moments of silence went for days. But after a minute, I decided it was time.

I held up one of the white linen napkins.

Me: Want to see a magic trick?

Girlfriend: No.

Well. That wasn't the answer I was looking for.

I tried again.

Me: C'mon. I want to show you a magic trick.

Girlfriend: I don't want to see a magic trick.

Seriously?

Me: Watch. I'm going to turn this napkin into a vegetable.

Girlfriend: I'm all set—*not even looking up from her menu*—No magic is necessary.

Oh for fuck's sake. Really?

In my head, this was how it was supposed to play out:

Me: *Want to see a magic trick?*

Girlfriend: *Oh yes! I would like nothing more than to see a magic trick, Rod! My, you look muscly, tonight.*

Me: *I'm going to turn this napkin into a vegetable.*

Girlfriend: *You are a god amongst men. Yes. Turn that napkin into a vegetable!*

Me: *(Waving hand over the napkin) Alacazam! Open it!*

She'd open it to find the diamond inside.

Me: *See? It's turned into a karat!*

Karat. Carrot. See what I did there?

And then I'd ask her to marry me, and she'd yell, "YES I WILL MARRY YOU, YOU AMAZING LOVE STALLION!" and the restaurant would erupt in applause. I'd be carried out on the shoulders of men while women would stare at me, fondling their ample breasts and moaning ever so slightly.

But no, here's how it actually went:

Me: OH COME ON. I'm showing you a magic trick.

Girlfriend: FINE.

I folded the napkin and held my hand over it.

Me: See? Normal napkin, right?

Girlfriend: Mmmhm.

I ran my hand over it a few times, and as I did, pushed the diamond ring up into it from beneath the table. Grasping the ring firmly with my hand over the napkin, I then rolled the napkin into a ball and held it out to her, my smile stretching from ear to ear.

Me: Go ahead. Open it.

Girlfriend: No.

Me: Open it. You'll see it's a vegetable!

Girlfriend: No.

Me: Please? Open it? Will you please open it?

Girlfriend: You open it.

Me: NO. You have to open it. That's the key to the trick an—

Girlfriend: *FINE.*

She snatched the napkin from my hands and flicked it open in one, fluid movement. I watched in slow motion horror as the ring launched 20 feet into the air and flew, ass-over-teakettle, over the heads of the couple sitting behind my girlfriend. Then it went over the heads of the table behind them, and the table behind them. It kept rising through the air like a shiny, lost balloon.

I tried to keep my eyes on it, but it was a tiny little thing. I heard the "tick" as it hit a table somewhere further down the restaurant, and then listened to the faint, sickening, scuttle as it landed and rattled across the floor.

My girlfriend looked at me in stunned shock realizing that she had, in fact, just chucked an expensive piece of jewelry across a crowded restaurant.

I would have reacted to her face with an "AYFKM" look, but I jumped up and rushed down the aisle trying to find the goddamn thing.

I scanned the floors but saw nothing except crumbs, dropped food, and dirt, and realized the restaurant was pretty disgusting. People pointed and said things like, "I think it went that way," but I still couldn't find the ring.

Then I realized everyone was pointing to an area near the corner of the knotty pine floor boards.

The knotty pine.

I glanced at the attractive woman sitting at the corner table I would now have to climb under and—OH SHE'S WEARING A DRESS maybe I can sneak a peek NO RODNEY, STAY THE COURSE and look for the ring.

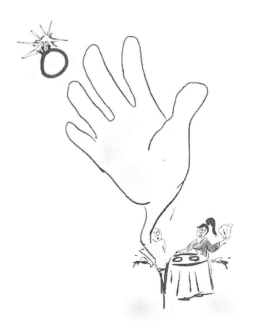

I felt like Gollum searching for that damn precious ring, which is a bit of foreshadowing because now—20 years later—I look a lot like him.

Time is cruel.

As I lifted the tablecloth, I saw it. Not the ring, mind you, but the knothole. The stupid, stupid knothole in the pine floor.

I tried to look into it, but there wasn't enough light.

Then I shot a look to the right to see if I could look up that lady's dress, but it was too dark there, too. I was having zero luck with EVERYTHING.

I reached into the knothole with a finger and felt the ring. Luckily, I have hands the size of a baby spider monkey, so after a bit of finagling, I was able to retrieve it.

I held it up, blew off the dust of 1,000 mozzarella sticks, and smiled at the lady trying to eat her lasagna.

I returned to my girlfriend and sat down, covered in dust and crumbs. "Here ya go," I said, placing the ring on the table.

She stared down at it, the diamond now encrusted in a fine layer of panko bits, then looked back at me, dumbfounded.

With as much disinterest as I could muster, I threw up some half-hearted jazz hands.

"Tadaaaa."

III. Repeat and Shuffle

"Most people, including myself, keep repeating the same mistakes." — **William Shatner**

My proposal to Kerri went a lot smoother than my "magic proposal." Had I been able to emulate Criss Angel during that fiasco, I would have used my powers to levitate right the hell out of the restaurant, saying, "Thee you later, thuckas!"

On that note, why can't he make *his lisp* disappear? Then I'd be impressed.

I'm not a serial husband. I've only proposed to women a few times, and been accepted twice. Two marriages is fine with me, because I like keeping most of my money when the relationship eventually goes south.

I considered writing a prenuptial agreement with Kerri, but then realized she can only take half of my current worth, which is roughly four cups of instant oatmeal and a dish rag.

I showed up at Kerri's with my daughter, and she answered the door in her oversized owl pajama shirt and a pair of sweats. I dropped to one knee and held out the ring box.

Suffice it to say, she said "yes" because I'm irresistible. Plus, my daughter was filming the entire thing, and no one wants to look like an asshole on YouTube.

We planned a small wedding with 20 or so extremely close friends. We chose the wine cellar of a local restaurant for the nuptials and reception because the close proximity of booze meant we were served faster.

Priorities change when you're on a second, third, or fourth marriage where

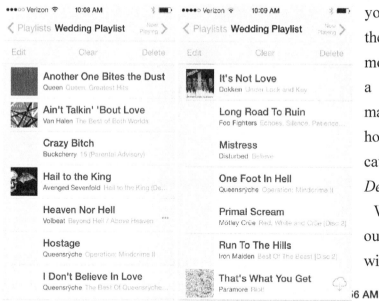

you think less about the function and more about getting a decent buzz and making sure you're home in time to catch *The Walking Dead.*

We could hook our iPods into the wine cellar's sound system, allowing us to play our own music, so I told Kerri I'd take care of the tunes. She countered by telling me she wanted to approve the playlists.

FINE.

I sent her the first playlist for the general reception (above).

It was quickly axed, as was my playlist for our first dance song choices (right).

> **Kerri:** Yeah. No. I think I'll take care of the playlists, thanks.

So the marriage was starting off on the wrong foot before it began.

 Beauty and the Beast (So...
Angela Lansbury Beauty and the Beast...

Feel So Numb
Rob Zombie The Sinister Urge

 Porn Star Dancing (feat. L...
My Darkest Days My Darkest Days (Bo...

Victimized
Linkin Park Living Things

Welcome To The Jungle
Guns N' Roses Appetite For Destruction

What I've Done
Linkin Park Minutes To Midnight

 The Duck Song
Bryant Oden The Duck Song (The Duck...

This did not bode well for the playlist of song suggestions I gave her for our honeymoon "activities":

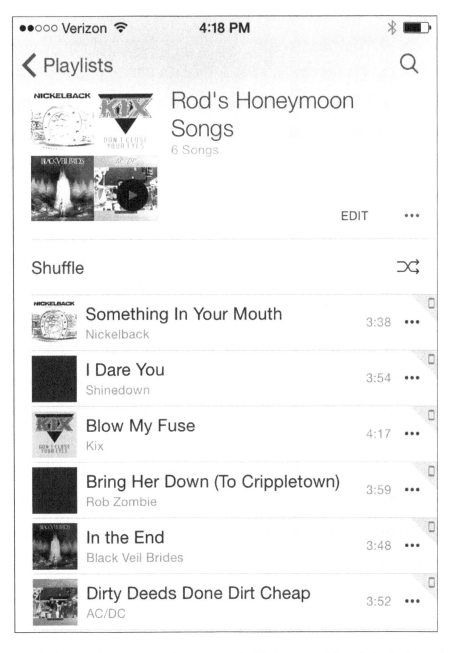

I thought it was ingenious. Of course, I think everything I do is ingenious. It's part of my charm, but gets old very quickly.

That's when Kerri countered with her own honeymoon playlist:

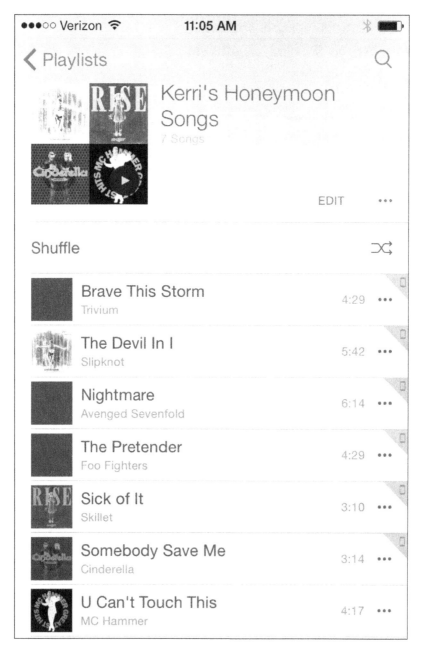

Touché, woman. Touché.

Although, that hurt a little if I'm being perfectly honest with you.

Our honeymoon playlist ended up like this:

As you can clearly see, this was a successful exercise in compromise.

I got to add in a bunch of filthy sex songs filled with innuendo and she got a bunch of licks in on how crappy I am in the sack. Overall, this is a win-win because bargaining and eventually giving in to the woman is one of the cornerstones of a lasting relationship. Failing to bargain with your mate could be considered the ultimate sin.

The Ultimate Sin.

Dammit. I should have added that to my playlist.

IV. The Really Shitty Honeymoon

I originally had this section in the "Wanna Get Away" portion of the relationship stories, and then decided it was best served here, in the marriage section of the book. You may disagree, however, after reading it.

shines flashlight under chin

The following is not for the faint of heart. You've been warned.

maniacal laugh causes coughing fit

If you're married, getting married, or already married, I present to you another one of the Getaways to Avoid:

Getaway to Avoid #3: Las Vegas

I can already hear the audible "gasp" coming from some of you right now, so let me clarify the title of this one:

Getaway to Avoid #3: Las Vegas, if you drink

There. Better.

My wife and I had been courting for nearly three years with only a single two-day getaway to show for it. This is because each of us has kids, and kids ruin everything. As a side note, please look for my next book called "I Love You, Now Go Away—A Book on Hands-Off Parenting."

After Kerri and I married in 2013, my mother bought us a honeymoon vacation for a wedding present: a 4-day, 3-night trip to Las Vegas. We were stunned and excited, mostly because (a) we were finally getting away from the children, and (b) that's pretty much the only reason.

So we packed our bags (including the "Kids Ruin Everything" t-shirt I had custom made) and headed to Sin City.

Las Vegas is overwhelmingly massive and beautiful, and you can drink booze outside. Being from New Hampshire, public intoxication without risk of arrest or being sexually assaulted by a moose was something new to us.

So naturally, we started pounding back the alcohol at 11 AM the morning after we arrived. We didn't feel the effects because you walk around SO MUCH, and thank God there are so many escalators, because by 5 PM, we'd ingested enough alcohol to sterilize surgical instruments just by peeing on them.

We both drank hard, so it was on or around 8 PM that things got really fuzzy. Here's what I remember from the rest of the night:

- Taking a cab to a strip joint, then making the cabbie drive us to a different one because the first one didn't serve alcohol. We needed a strip club that served booze because we'd only been drinking for ten hours straight.
- My wife vomiting on a stripper.
- Two strippers holding my wife's hair in the bathroom while I tried to take out money to buy more lap dances for myself, because those are my priorities.
- Getting kicked out of a cab on the ride back to the hotel.
- Standing by my wife while she slumped on the sidewalk of a seedy back road, screaming, "I DON'T WANT TO DIE HERE."

The blackout happened shortly thereafter, although I do remember trying to help my wife get through the crowd in the lobby of The Paris Hotel, her arm hung limply over my shoulder while I dragged her around like I was having a weekend at Bernie's. But instead of Bernie, it was my semi-conscious wife with a blood alcohol content of 85-proof.

It was around then my brain shut down. The wave of alcohol washed over my body and completely drowned me. I literally felt like I was underwater, with wave upon wave of water pelting me in a sea of ... a sea of ...

Jesus H. Christ. What was that god-awful smell?

I cracked the slits of my eyes open, and I found that I was, indeed, being pelted with water. I turned my head to get my bearings and realized I was seated on the beautiful tile floor of the glass-walled shower in our hotel room. Through the steamy glass, I could see my wife unconscious on our bed.

I started to push myself up, but my hand went *WHOOP* right out from under me. My body crashed to the shower floor. I opened my eyes once more, and saw the source of the odor.

There, a scant two inches from my face, was a poop.

A POOP.

I bolted upright, my eyes wide open for the first time since my third margarita at noon-ish.

Poop everywhere.

Poop on the floor. Poop on the glass walls. Of course, people with ADD still have ADD when they're completely blotto, so Pink Floyd lyrics floated through my head:

"All in all it's just a-nother poop on the wall ..."

I laughed at my joke and slapped my knee.

SPLAT.

There was poop on ME. OHMYGOD THERE IS POOP ON ME.[1]

In my defense, I'm not sure whose feces I was covered in. I have zero idea if I pooped myself or my wife pooped on me or if it was mutual or an accident.

Where did it come from? Actually, the question was more of WHO did it come from?

I thought back to the dawn of woo and thought maybe, just maybe, this was

---

[1] Editor's Note: This would not be a Rodney Lacroix book without a poop story.

my wife giving me her own version of caveman chocolates. But there were no accompanying feathers. No dead sloth.

Nope. This was just plain ol' regular feces.

I stopped questioning whose it was—maybe I paid a stripper for it—and focused more on removing it, and maybe peeling off all my skin while I was at it.

Thank God I was in the shower because that made for easy rinsing, even though I don't think I could ever shower enough. The fact there was no "Boil You Alive" temperature setting on the shower head didn't help.

As an aside, shower steam + caca smell is what I assume 3-week old zombies smell like. Add in the aroma of the 15 times I retched while trying to wash it off, and you can see how that night had become my own personal episode of Fear Factor.

Also, we are not allowed back to The Paris ever again as long as we live.

We spent the next two days in Vegas sick to our stomachs, confined to our hotel rooms, and unable to eat anything without hurling. I think the only place we managed to venture was Madame Tussaud's Wax Museum, which by the way, has its own bar because God forbid you go anywhere in Vegas without vomiting.

We returned home with our livers severely damaged, but still intact, and headed over to my mom's house to pick up my dog.

Mom: Have fun?

Me: Um. Yeah. Mainly.

Mom: Great. For your next trip, I was thinking of getting you a weekend in New Orleans.

I swear that woman is trying to kill us.

Act 6 Progress Checklist

Wow. Sure were a lot of feel-good moments in that section, eh? The bottom line is that marriage isn't for everyone. And for some, it's a multiple-time occurrence. Whether or not you decide to tie the knot, and therefore, tie your genitals in knots, make the situation fun for the both of you, and for the love of all that's holy, stop drinking in Vegas by noon.

	Yes	No
Chicks dig magic.	☐	☒
Proposing to someone using a magic trick is an amazingly good idea.	☐	☒
I should have juggled instead.	☑	☐
Brides love when grooms make up the wedding playlists.	☐	☒
Iron Maiden is awesome.	☑	☐
Vegas is more fun when you've been drinking for 12 hours straight and only weigh 140 pounds.	☐	☒
You could have done without the feces visual.	☑	☐

Act 7 - Parental Guidance

The Bucket List Tips Over

Voiceover: We now return to our theatrical production format.

The curtain opens to a living room setting. A lone woman sits on the sofa and faces the audience as she stares down at a box in her left hand. Her gaze switches from the box to an object she's holding in her other hand, and then back to the box again. The audience can't see what the other object is.

The fake stage door opens, and a man walks in.

"All set!" he exclaims. "Got the tickets. We leave Saturday!"

The woman looks up and smiles at him.

"CANCUN, BABY!" he tries again.

The woman smiles and looks at the object in her hands again.

"Woo? Hello?"

Nothing. No response. He hangs his coat and sidles up beside her on the couch.

"What's wrong?" he asks.

She hands him the object she has been holding. It's a small white stick. He looks at it, puzzled, and then grabs the box from her other hand. His face changes from confusion to shock, and he leaps from the couch.

"ARE YOU PREGNANT?!"

She nods.

The audience isn't sure if the couple should be happy or sad. If you think they should be happy, let's go with that. If you think they should drop down to their knees, look up at the sky, and scream, "Whyyyyyy?!" then go with that.

Either way, I'm not here to judge you ...

The couple finishes their (kissing/handshake/high-fiving/sobbing) and the man takes out his cell phone. It's a flip phone because he's cheap and has never known the hypnotic draw and frustration of Flappy Bird. The audience silently envies him.

He dials a number and waits for the other end to answer.

"Um, yes, hi," he starts, "I was just in there picking up my tickets for Cancun."

He pauses a second.

"I'm going to need to cancel that trip."

He hangs up the phone, and walks over to the counter. He picks up a jar filled with hundreds of folded scraps of paper and walks over to a closet. We see that the jar reads: Our Bucket List.

He opens the closet door and slides it far back on a top shelf. He turns to find the woman putting another container on the counter.

It reads: *Our Family Bucket List*.

She writes something on a scrap of paper and folds it. He takes it from her and drops it inside.

Lights dim. Curtain closes.

Fin.

I. Kid Stuff

A number of people suggested I write a section about how to keep romance alive when you have children. I happen to have two biological children and two step-children. They're called "step-children" because you can stand on them to help you reach things on high shelves at the grocery store with little to no harm done to your own kids.

I'll probably lose custody after this book hits the shelves.

On the next few pages are some ideas of how to keep romance alive if you have kids.

Enjoy.

This page intentionally left blank.

This page intentionally left blank.

II. Kid Stuff (continued)

Okay, just messing with you.

It's actually not that difficult to kindle romance when there are children pestering you constantly. There are ways even if you have to help a four-year-old wipe poop off her bum at 3 AM, or are exhausted from screaming at your teenager to take off the damn headphones—IF YOU CAN'T HEAR ME WHEN I'M YELLING THEN YOUR HEADPHONES ARE UP TOO LOUD.

There's a reason why I'm not a spokesman for in-vitro fertilization companies.

In a rare and serious note, I've always believed it's more important for children to see their mother or father in a loving, nurturing relationship than to be involved in one where the parents show little to no regard for each other. The bottom line is, if you hear, "EW, GROSS," from your children a lot, you're on the right track.

So, now I'll give you some ideas of how you can include your kids in your romantic endeavors. This sounds gross and that was not my intent. Let me rephrase it by saying it's easy to incorporate your children into gifts of love for your spouse or partner.

I'm not making it any better. Let's just get to the stories and let them speak for themselves. I SAID LET THEM SPEAK FOR THEMSELVES.

Seriously, honey. Turn the headphones down.

III. So Much Head

The content of this story isn't what you think it is. I'm saving that for my picture book of sex positions. It's like *The Kama Sutra* except all the positions illustrated are just me, alone, curled into a fetal position.

There's a reason no literary agents have contacted me yet.

Let's begin...

Kerri: Ummm. Is it supposed to be really scary?

That, my friends, is not the reaction I was shooting for as she opened my gift. I expected some kissing with lots of tongue action. Maybe even a little nookie. At the very least, some dry humping. But instead, there was confusion.

Now let's go back to the very beginning...

Kerri and I had been together for a while, so I wanted to do something special that reflected our relationship. It was Valentine's Day. I had already given her a sweet interpretive dance of "Wind Beneath My Wings" for Christmas, and getting her a teddy bear was totally out of the question after what I learned by following the flowchart depicted in an earlier chapter.

With little time to spare, and the holiday coming close, I racked my brains for an amazing gift.[1] I searched my memory for thoughtful presents I'd received in the past, and figured I'd do the "pay it forward" thing and recycle the idea with my own twist.

After nixing a tee-shirt with my face on it, a singing fish mounted on a

---

[1] This one sentence took ten minutes to write because there are a lot of different opinions on whether the saying should be 'racked my brain' or 'wracked my brain.' Eventually, I decided it wasn't worth giving a shit and used the first one.

plaque, and a mug that says, "Coffee Makes Me Poop," I felt like giving up.

That's when it dawned on me: I'll MAKE HER A PICTURE COLLAGE.[1]

95% of male readers throw book into fireplace

I have a few framed photo collections, showing me and my children, which were given to me in the past. There's one of me with my daughter. There's another of me with my son. And a third of me with both of my kids.

Then I found a weird collage in mom's attic where I'm posed with strange men in a late 70s disco. I don't like that one.

I decided that two nice picture projects—one from Kerri's children and one from me—would be great gift ideas.

Kerri and I had been to our share of places and parties and dark, underground sex dungeons, so we had plenty of photos of us in various situations. If you're a close friend of ours, you may have received some of these situational photos in a random text at 2 AM on a Saturday morning. You're welcome.

I decided I would make her kids' collage first, which required me to go through her Facebook timeline and pull down pictures from her children's birth until the most recent.

That was easy because I'm always stalking her timeline anyway, and seriously, who is this "Buster" guy who keeps commenting on her posts, and how does he know she likes ice cubes so much?

Sorry.

Download and print.

Download and print.

---

[1] A collage is a collection of images not unlike most ransom notes but with a lesser chance of a felony conviction.

Download and print.

Pownload and drint.

Porn loads in dirt.

I made it through three pictures before I got confused and distracted. Then I spent the next 20 minutes looking at internet image search results for "porn loads and dirt."

And now so have you. Good luck explaining that browser history to your spouse.

I began the critical process of cutting up the photos. I call this the "critical" task because I was almost out of printer paper and forgot to buy more. I blame the porn-dirt tangent I went off on earlier. So, yes, I needed to get the cutting right the very first time.

I have a degree in Architecture, and there is a saying amongst our secret society that goes: "Measure twice, cut once." There might be something in that saying relevant to my point here, but there's a reason I'm hocking crappy books on the internet and not building skyscrapers and taking bikini models to Ruth's Chris Steakhouse every night.

Great, now I'm sad I didn't pay more attention in Architecture School.

takes bite out of Hot Pocket

I spent hours downloading and cutting up pictures of her and her children. I tried to avoid a lot of baby pictures because babies are gross. I've also previously established in this book that old people are gross, too. The sweet spot for attractive people is from 20 to 45, so if you're going to do this project, aim for photos in that age period.

Yes, I am fully aware that I fall outside of that range, but I've made my peace with it.

a lonely hair drifts down and lands on keyboard

I arranged the picture pieces on the cardboard backing of the frame I bought. I tried to place the pictures with straight edges along the sides because that seemed to make sense to me. Maybe my parents' investment in college wasn't in vain after all.

Then I took the pictures that were cut irregularly or in heart shapes and filled in all the gaps. When it was done, I held the frame up and watched all the pictures fall out because I forgot to tape them on.

On second thought, I should start paying my parents back on those student loans.

I ran to the closet and grabbed a hot glue gun. I figured that would be better instead of tape after realizing all the tape was in the basement with the wrapping paper, and it's scary down there.

I squeezed out the first glop of glue on the frame and stuck a picture to it. The glue immediately oozed through the picture, fucking the whole thing up and morphing the baby's face into *The Scream* by Edvard Munch.

Great. Now I'm going to have to go get tape from the basement and probably die at the hands of a monster or something. Just because I'm a black-belt doesn't mean I'm not afraid of Freddy Krueger, people.

After 36 shoulder-rolls and yelling, "I HAVE A GUN," six times, I successfully retrieved a roll of tape and bolted back up the cellar stairs at 648 miles per hour. The lesson here is to use tape from the beginning and avoid being killed in your cellar. Also, if you use a glue gun you'll booger up the pictures.

"Don't booger up the pictures." — **Rodney Lacroix, 2015**

I taped the remainder of the photos to the cardboard backing, trying to figure out where the crap I'd them placed originally.

The end result was this:

Sweeeeet, right?

I turned my attention to the collage gift that would be from me. I planned on making something very similar, except with pictures of only us—instead of ruining it with children. If you don't have kids, this sounds cruel. If you do have kids, you're thinking, "Yep."

Sure, we have a lot of photos of us together, but most associate with stories that evoke the question, "Do you remember how sick we got that night?" After sorting through all our pictures for good memories, I was left with only two decent ones, so I decided to download all of them anyway.

Remember: Quantity over Quality.

I ran out of paper so I copied the pictures to a thumb drive and drove down to the local pharmacy to print them out as real photos. I also had my Viagra prescription refilled while I was there because I was sooooo gonna get laid after giving these collages.

It's always good to be prepared for situations like this. Before you refill that prescription, though, make sure the project comes out looking really good. You don't want to pop a Viagra and then *not* get laid, because you'll be stuck trying to masturbate a four-hour erection away.

My right arm is massive.

I was about a quarter of the way into cutting up the pictures when I realized I should have bought a larger frame. I had way too many photos, and the frame was much smaller than the one I'd used in the first collage. I had to cut the pictures a little closer so I could fit them all in while trying to make sure the whole thing didn't look like caca poopoo.

You never want to hand over caca poopoo to the one you love. This sounds like it should be a song:

> *You know you were meant for me,*
>
> *You and I fit like a glove.*
>
> *But I screwed up making this collage.*
>
> *And gave caca poopoo to the one I love.*

So I performed scissor sorcery to pack as many photographic memories as I could into the smaller frame. While I'm on the subject of music, "Scissor Sorcery" sounds like a bad-ass band name.

"..and now here's Caca Poopoo Love Collage by Scissor Sorcery on America's Top 40 ... "

I finished the collage, wrapped it up, and stuffed it under the bed—the default location for all presents hidden in my house. It's not uncommon to find my bed teeter-tottering atop a four-foot pile of presents during holidays.

On the morning of Valentine's Day, I gave her the gifts.

She opened the one from her children first, tearing up with emotion as soon as she saw it.

She cried. A lot. Mainly because I slipped while handing it to her and stabbed her in the arm with the frame corner, but whatever.

But, as I thought she would, she loved the collage.

Then she opened mine. Once again, her face filled with emotion but this time it was more like this expression:

Kerri: Ummm. Is it supposed to be really scary?

Scary? Why is it scary? It's romantic and thoughtful and sweet. Those are usually the opposite of scary unless you're dating a Scientologist.

Me: You don't like it?

She looked up at me with a quizzical expression, wondering if I was asking her the question in all seriousness. Then, slowly, she turned the frame towards me as if I had no idea what I had given her, and she would be showing it to me for the first time.

And I saw the horror:

GAH.

SO MANY HEADS.

I didn't realize exactly how creepy it had turned out. I had crammed so many photos into the small 11"x14" frame that it looked like an aerial shot of a mannequin head factory. I cannot overstate how disturbing this picture was as I looked at it—*really looked at it*—for the first time.

Me: Oh my God, I'm so sorry. Happy Valentine's Day?

The picture, thankfully, never made it to a wall. It sits on my nightstand, a stark reminder of how easily things can go from an awesome idea to terrifying nightmare.

Speaking of nightmares, good luck sleeping after seeing that.

I know I'm going to be up all night.

One more word on this

I've done this particular project quite a bit, but I'm not talking about making collages just for girlfriends or wives. This idea can be, and was, used for any of the following:

- Christmas presents for grandparents
- Mother's Day (pictures of mom with the kids)
- Father's Day (pictures of dad with the kids)
- Stepmother's Day (pictures of stepmom making the kids mop the floor)
- Stepfather's Day (picture of stepfather locked in a room, drinking straight from a whiskey bottle while sitting in a recliner with headphones on)

Just make sure you don't cut the pictures too close. No one deserves a present that scary.

IV. The Ten-Second Rule

A Clip-N-Save Section

I thought I'd break rank for a bit and give some useful romance advice to parents, or to people who may be dating one. If you're dating a mom or dad, just make sure it's not my mom because I will have to kill you.

In this section are a bunch of stories and tips about how to get the kids involved in your expressions of love. There are times, though, when you want the kids to just go the hell away.

Seriously, give us, like, 30 seconds alone so I can say hi to your mom and—

FINE. FINE. I'll get you a juice box. Jesus.

If your family is anything like mine, you may find it difficult to get any time away from the kids at all. In our house, there can be four children running amok at any given time.

FOUR.

There is an eight-year age difference between the oldest and youngest, which equates to a lot of yelling and brain aneurysms. It's also the reason why I've had to reinforce the shelving of my liquor cabinet.

So finding some "couple time" in a situation like this can be challenging.

In blended families[1], this hardship can be compounded by things like custody agreements and shitty exes who keep bailing on their own children.

---

[1] A "blended family" is not a family that has been mixed with fruit juices and yogurt in a food processor. That is a "smoothie family" and is the energy drink of choice for cannibals doing CrossFit.

Or maybe you can't break free because of the lack of sexy babysitters at your disposal, or your work schedules are hectic.

Whatever the reason, it sucks. So here are some ideas you can use as a couple to show each other you're still interested, even though the children are slowly draining your sanity.

All these ideas take ten seconds or less. That's all the time you usually have, so they fit in perfectly.

Find time to dance

Your wife is running around the kitchen, packing snacks and filling drinks. Stop her, grab her, and dance with her. If she yells, "I can't now," reply with, "Give me ten seconds," which you say to her every Saturday night, anyway. Then, just dance.

Slow dance. Don't do the Electric Slide. That's weird. Also, if you know the Electric Slide you may have other issues, dude.

Grab a cheek

Passing her by in the hallway? Grab a butt cheek.

She's bent over looking for something in the fridge? Grab a butt cheek.

Picking something up off the floor? Butt cheek.

She's complaining about the Mexican food she had last night? HOLD OFF RIGHT NOW.

Butt grabs are fun, and the best part, they're fly-by-night, so you don't have to worry about making time to do it.

Kiss a cheek

She's bent over looking for someth—

Whoops. Wrong cheek.

Whatever she's doing, run over and give her a kiss on the cheek. She may not have time, or thanks to the hummus she had for lunch, she might not have the best breath in the world. There's no need to jump into a full make-out session. A peck on the cheek sends a quick and easy message.

The message might be, "Please stop eating things so heavy on the garlic," but whatever.

Sit next to each other

This is a really tough one at my house, because with six bodies there at any given time, seating space is a premium in the living room. I've tried to institute "Reserved Seating," but it didn't work, primarily because my kids never have enough cash on them, and they're too young for credit cards.

If you can manage, make sure you get the prime seats next to each other during family television time. Holding hands wouldn't hurt, either, because it will gross the kids out, and maybe they'll want to go to bed early. Anything that has the potential for sending the kids to bed early is well worth a shot.

Get a bedroom door lock

I shouldn't have even had to put that there.

Bottom line

I've been through divorce, and every therapist will tell you that how a child sees their parents treating each other is the most influential factor on how they will someday treat their own romantic relationships. I don't get serious a lot in this book, but I'm serious here. Keep this in mind if you have kids in your house and you want them to have healthy relationships in the future. That is, if you don't kill them by then.

V. Karaohhhhhke

"I love music videos, I really do. I think it's kind of sad that it's a dying art form." — **Adam Levine**

"I can never unsee this." — **my kids, after I showed them the video for my hit single, "I Got Bouncy Bouncy Moobs"**

NOTE: For best effect, read this next section like a voice-over guy selling a CD compilation.

Music videos.

We've all seen them. Remember watching a hot and sexy Tawny Kitaen writhe around the hood of a Jaguar while the old guy from the Six Flags Amusement Park commercials put on a wig and sang to her?

You do? Jesus. How old are you? It's 4 PM, shouldn't you be eating dinner at Denny's?

Remember watching Miley Cyrus ride that wrecking ball while she licked a hammer? Or remember trying really, really hard to forget watching Miley Cyrus ride that wrecking ball while she licked a hammer?

If you can think of any music video, you can also recollect the feelings it gave you while you watched it. Like "horny" for Tawny Kitaen or "repulsed" for Miley. Seriously, I'd rather watch the Six Flags guy riding around on that damn ball.

Great. Now I'm horny.

Well, YOU TOO can instill those very same feelings in your lover by making—yes, making—your very own music video.

End voice-over

A word of caution before you execute this one:

You will either become the greatest romantic for years to come, or the butt of jokes for all time. If done correctly, though, this fun project will fall somewhere between the two.

What we are going to do is extremely simple and fun. However, this assumes you have zero qualms about making a complete ass out of yourself or—if applicable—your children. Making a fool out of myself is ingrained in my DNA, so this project was a walk in the park. If you're an introvert, or have trouble standing in front of a camera and belting out a Celine Dion tune, this may not be the project for you.

Since this is in the "romantic ideas inclusive to children" section, I'm going to assume you have some. If you don't, then go buy[1] or borrow someone else's to become your "backup band" for the video, because (a) it's hysterical, and (b) it's hysterical. Also (c) it's heartwarming, and warming hearts is what this book is all about. It's also about me making enough profit for a Mercedes down payment.

At the time I made my video, my kids were 4 and 7 years old. They are 11 and 14 now, and have evolved into beings who ignore direction and are half-human/half-earbud.

I told my kids to go find as much of their outrageous dress-up clothes as they could. POOF—off they went to rummage through bins and buckets and cubby holes and dumpsters and maybe squat houses. My parenting style is pretty much "hands off."

---

[1] I am not condoning the illegal purchase of children for the purposes of making a music video. Mainly because most kids don't come with a receipt, so you can only exchange them for another one of lesser or equal value. Such a rip-off.

While they were gone, I found my wedding song on the karaoke channel of my cable provider.

FANTASTIC.

I played it through once, realizing I knew none of the words because it wasn't sung by Iron Maiden. In retrospect, I would choose their song "Running Free" as an anthem if there was such a thing as a divorce reception, and yes, I would sing it flawlessly.

I turned the webcam of my computer on and aimed it into the living room, where I could stand in the middle, still look at the webcam, AND see the television out of the corner of my eye. I thumbtacked a large blue blanket to the ceiling as the "backdrop."

I wanted to create a "studio" feel, but my dog kept running in and out of the frame and even stopped to lick herself once. SERIOUSLY I'M TRYING TO MAKE A VIDEO, DOG.

My children returned from their scavenger hunt with a treasure trove of dress-up stuff:

- A feather boa.
- Some oversized sunglasses.
- A wig.

Seriously, a wig. Why do my kids have wigs? Never mind. I don't want to know.

I pulled off my son's shirt and put the oversized sunglasses on him. My daughter got the feather boa and another pair of sunglasses. I set her up in front of the toy keyboard over to the side, and of course, I gave my son the inflatable guitar. There he was: 30 inches tall, shirtless, wearing giant sunglasses, and holding a balloon guitar. It looked as amazing as it sounds.

If you don't have kids you're thinking, "Why the Hell do they have an inflatable guitar?" but if you have children, you're saying to yourself, "FINALLY A PURPOSE FOR THE INFLATABLE GUITAR." Trust me on this one. I have so much inflatable crap in my house I'm surprised the whole building hasn't floated away yet.

I posed my kids in front of the blanket, made sure the webcam had us all in the frame, and started rolling.

I gave a short introduction before hitting "PLAY" on the karaoke song, and the three of us let it rip. I sang my guts out as my son and daughter swayed to the music and fake-played their instruments. It was nothing short of hysterical, horrifying, and astonishing all at once.

If I have one regret, it's that I let my son do the shirtless-sunglass-look instead of me.

Just two takes later, it was done.

The resulting video, copied onto DVD, provided both an incredible laugh and an amazing keepsake. And it helped cement my place in the lore of all things romantic when I gave it to my wife as an anniversary present.

This idea is a one-and-done type of gift because it's hard to recreate the surprise and majesty of the first time you give someone a video of you and your children singing karaoke love songs. You can't reinvent the magic with a video of you rolling around on the hood of a Jaguar or sitting on a giant exercise ball dressed like Miley Cyrus. Don't ask me how I know this.

Go. Have fun. Let loose. Footloose.

Great. Now I have that song in my head.

All I need is an empty warehouse and a tractor, and I'm totally making my wife a video.

VI. Wanna Get Away from the Bellhop?

A lot of parents have the luxury of living near close family. This means they can usually rely on them when they need a couples getaway for a weekend or week or month or forever.

God, that sounds nice.

Most times, though, a romantic getaway for parents means hiring a sitter for two hours while you run out for a nice dinner. But, there's a 90-minute wait at the restaurant, so you eat a quick chimichanga at *TGI Friday's* because the sitter charges $20 an hour, and you don't want to take out a second mortgage.

When I was a child, my parents would put me in a closet with lots of pillows, a bowl of water, and some kibble. The 70s were a much simpler time.

Taking a romantic vacation as a couple is a daunting task. It's usually difficult to convince the grandparents to watch your children for longer than four hours. Their secondary task as grandparents is to criticize your parenting skills from afar.

As such, you're typically stuck with dragging the kids along on your vacations. What was once a weekend trip to Hedonism is now a 3-day jaunt to Sesame Place.

Sure there are still people in costumes, but it's a totally different vibe now, and *this* Elmo will have you thrown out if you tickle him in the wrong spot.

It was during one of those needs for a getaway, with no one willing to babysit our monsters, that I looked for a road-trip vacation for the entire family. Of course, we'd hit the usual kid-friendly places, but I wanted to end the trip in Toronto, where our beloved Boston Red Sox would be playing the Blue Jays during the last few days of our trip. Nothing says "family fun" like listening to kids whine through a 3-hour ball game, so the timing was perfect.

It's tough to find a hotel when you're traveling with kids. It's not like you have to worry about having sex in the same hotel room as them, because sex stopped as soon as the kids were born.

It's more a comfort thing, because one parent (dad) always ends up sleeping on a sofa while the kids sleep in the cushy bed with the other parent (mom). The sofa is lumpy and smells, so the couch-parent hits the bar at 2:30 AM and sings karaoke with Chinese businessmen.

The cheapest rates I could get for the Toronto hotel I found were coupled with a "Romance Package." This intrigued me, because "Romance Package" is the pet name for my genitals. I looked a little further into this because it was a lot less expensive than a room without the offer.

Your Romance Package Includes:
- Two splits of sparkling wine.
- Valet parking.
- A sumptuous welcome treat at check-in.
- A Massage Oil and "Love Kit."

Shhhh—*presses finger to lips*—You had me at "valet parking."

I was sold. I had no idea what a split of wine was, because *TGI Friday's* only sells wine by the plastic glass (unless by "split" they're talking about the seam running up the side of the goblet).

I also had no idea what a "Love Kit" was; it sounded like something I'd have to put together, so no thank you, hotel. But "sumptuous treat" usually means "free cookie" so ...

books room

We arrived at the hotel and checked in. They handed me the key to the room, and the entire family shuffled into the elevator with our 14 bags, three pillows (because kids can't travel without their own pillow for some reason), and 76 stuffed animals.

I'd also brought two cases of Ibuprofen and bottle of Jack Daniels to help me cope.

We settled into the room and as I looked around, I realized a few things:

- We did not receive our "sumptuous treat" at check-in.
- There was no wine in the room.
- We were sans the promised Massage Oil and "Love Kit."

I'd been robbed of my trinkets!

I immediately called down to the front desk.

> **Me:** Hi. My room was supposed to come with the "Romance Package," but I didn't get my wine or sumptuous treat.
>
> **Front desk:** I'm sorry. We'll have someone bring that right up. Did you at least receive the "Love Kit?"
>
> **Me:** No—*whispering because the kids were right behind me*—No Love Kit, either.

I whispered it because (a) I didn't want my kids to start questioning what a "Love Kit" was when even I didn't know, and (b) I had already answered enough questions for the entire trip.

For example, I had to explain to the kids that "Toronto" was an old Iroquois term that meant "City of Homelessness that Smells of Urine."[1]

I wish I was kidding about the million questions, but by the time we reached our hotel, I had said, "This is why you stay in school," about 100 times.

I hung up the phone and leaned back on the lumpy couch. Everyone was already getting comfortable after the day's long drive, and it was kind of late, so I went back into the bedroom and put on my silk pajama shorts:

---

[1] *Toronto* actually means "Where there are trees in water," but by "trees" I think they mean "people" and by "water" they mean "alleys."

When you're married and have kids, boxers like this are a great way to tell the world that you've given up.

Someone knocked at the door.

Shirtless and wearing only the sexy pajama-wear you see above, I answered. It was a bellhop.

In his hands he held a bottle of wine, a heart-shaped box of bonbons, and a rectangular, black box. On the box I could see several figures depicted in Japanese art, all in Kama Sutra-type positions.

In large, bold red letters on the box were the easily readable words:

<u>Your Sensual Kit Contains:</u>

Edible body powder, Scented massage oil, Flavored Shower Gel, and an Erotic Feather Tickler.

Awesome.

The bellhop took a second to look me up and down. Then, slowly, a smirk crept over his face.

It was the cheeky smirk of a man who realized I was about to get my super freak on, and I was the type of guy to take that erotic feather tickler an—

"Who's that, daddy?" my daughter yelled from the other room.

The bellhop's face immediately melted from "Ooooh yeah" to "OH GOD," not unlike the Nazis at the end of *Raiders of the Lost Ark.*

I looked up from the dirty box of sex he was holding and met his gaze. I blinked.

cricket

I grabbed the stuff out of his hand as quickly as I could and blurted out, "Thank you." I shut the door in his face just as my daughter appeared.

"Who was that?" she asked again.

"No one," I answered. "Who wants chocolates?"

VII. Throwing Paint

"Painting is silent poetry, and poetry is painting that speaks." — **Plutarch**

"See? It looks like a lighthouse when I'm in the bathtub." — **me, age 7, explaining to my mom why I used her nail polish to paint my genitals white with red stripes**

I'm realizing, maybe a little too late, that all the titles in this "Kid Section" are closer to sexual innuendo than any other place in this book. I really hope this is coincidence and not an indication of deeper issues.

knocks on wood

I originally came up with this chapter's idea after realizing the house we had just moved into had a bare wall that needed some sort of artwork on it. Normally, I don't care for art or understand it, as per this conversation with my son one day while walking past an art museum:

> **Son:** I don't understand half the stuff they call "art." It all looks like a mess.
>
> **Me:** That's because art is subjective.
>
> **Son:** What does "subjective" mean?
>
> **Me:** Stupid.

Blank walls indicate that your feng shui is feng-shitty, and despite my lack of artistic understanding, I decided our blank wall needed some special art only our family could create.

A project like this not only gets the kids involved, but it is so amazingly fun and versatile that you can do it as a gift for any of the following occasions:

- Birthdays.
- Anniversaries.
- Mother's Day.
- Father's Day.
- Grandparent's Day.
- Talk Like a Pirate Day.
- National Cheesecake Day.
- Now I'm Just Making Things Up Day.

I've even done this project for myself. Then myself and I had an amazing romantic dinner and watched *Silver Linings Playbook* before retiring to bed where we had a very intimate 23 seconds together. Sometimes I should stop writing while I'm ahead.

I thought a "family art wall" would be an awesome gift idea for Kerri, mainly because I bought too much paint.

Then I thought, *Why not do art for other rooms too?*

Yeah, way too much of this:

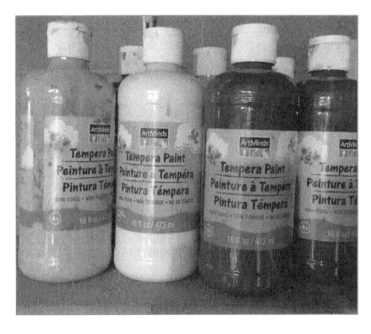

Thank goodness they write "Tempera Paint" in three different languages on the bottles because this book may go International, and I'd hate for Spanish people looking at this to go, "El Whato?" which is how I assume Spanish people say "what."

I only went to college for the booze.

A project like this takes zero skill, which is great, because the only artistic talents I have are Photoshopping myself into Kate Upton pictures, pasting the photos onto paper along with cutout magazine letters, and sending them to her in envelopes spritzed with Axe Body Spray (Phoenix).

I also like to doodle on the restraining orders she has sent back.

I hung a huge drop-cloth in my basement, propped a couple of canvases in front of it, set up a table for the paints, and called the kids. As they walked down the stairs, I greeted them with ponchos and rubber gloves.

The look of terror on their faces was worth it.

> **TIP:** If you try this idea, get yourself a poncho and some rubber gloves. You may already have these if your tequila nights are anything like mine. Also, pick up some painting sponges and brushes while you're buying the canvas at the art store. You can always use the sponges and brushes for sex night if you end up not doing this project. Maybe run to the grocery store and pick up some chocolate syrup, too.

Once again, I feel I've digressed.

First, I needed to decide on a theme for the paintings. I asked myself a few questions:

- What rooms will these go in?
- What occasion is this for?
- Who is it going to? Are they gothic? If so, do I have enough black paint?
- Why is my dog scratching at the carpet?

Sorry. My dog was just scratching at the carpet. I have no idea why, and I usually end up typing whatever I'm thinking.

I decided the bigger canvas would be for the family room. That room has a dark red fireplace, beige walls, black leather furniture, and *ohmygod* my dog is still scratching, wtf. Sorry.

It's very distracting.

The other painting was going to be for Kerri as a Valentine's Day gift. Unfortunately the kids were down here with me, so there went my idea of drawing a big dick and balls on it.

I'll have to come down and add that in subliminal undertones later, I thought.

We donned the ponchos, rubber gloves, and goggles, then dumped the paint in bowls, and started throwing paint.

Yes. We dipped our hands in the bowls of paint and chucked it at the canvases.

Flick. Whap. Whapflick. Flickwhap.

KAAAAAAAAAAAAAHHHHHHHNNNNNNN!

Whenever I get excited I yell "KAHN!" and throw my clenched fists in the air. It's almost a reflex.

We had a blast. When we got tired of using our fingers, we used paintbrushes. When we got tired of using paintbrushes, we used sponges.

Then my son stuck his butt in paint and made a butt print. Then we had to cover the butt print. No one wants a butt print painting. Then my daughter made a butt print. Screw it.

Everyone gets a butt print on their painting. The king has spoken.

We stopped every once in a while to turn the canvas 90 degrees because things all started to go in one direction. Also, everything is better when it's rotating.

wink

Of course, the kids made handprints and drew hearts and smiley faces on the family room painting. On my wife's canvas, I wrote things like "love" and "mine" and "4eva" and drew hearts (*and tiny hidden penises, shhhh*).[1]

When we were done, we had killed a ton of time and done something really

---

[1] True story: After my wife read the first draft of this, she spent 20 minutes looking for subliminal penises in her painting. Also, "Subliminal Penises" would be a great name for a band.

fun. Parenting is all about killing time until the kids are old enough to move out, so this project was a step in the right direction.

Here is the very Valentine's Day painting we made for my wife:

I made the base coat pink and wrote words you can pick out if you look for them. You have to squint to find some. You can see handprints of the children as well, although they look more like Wilson in *CastAway*.

There are also a lot of heart shapes, and I may or may not have subliminally wrote in phrases such as "I like to watch" in there. I'll never tell.

Kerri loved it and hung it in the hallway outside of our bedroom, so she sees it every time she wakes up after a night of snoring like Godzilla.

Seriously, it's almost inhuman.

I like that the painting is the first thing she sees whenever she leaves the room. I think she does, too. I don't know, I haven't asked her. I'm too tired because she keeps me up all night. It's nuts.[1]

BONUS: My "Better Than a Chia Pet" Birthday Idea

When Kerri was about to turn 40 (sorry honey, cat's out of the bag) a few years ago (I'm making it way worse now, aren't I?), I threw a huge bash. She knew about the party, but didn't know the trouble I went through to make it memorable.

One of the things I had planned to make this party something special was to have each of the birthday guests go into the basement one at a time (or in couples) and take turns making her gift:

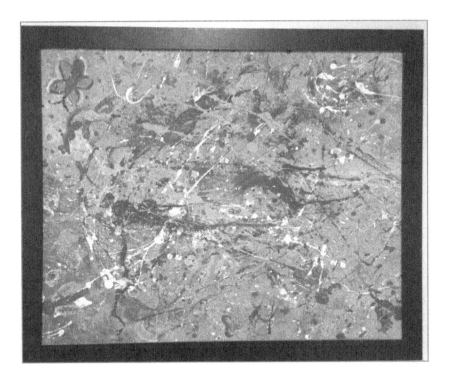

---

[1] I know what you're thinking at this point. For a book on Romance Tips, I'm really digging into my wife here for the snoring thing. With that being said, it's one of the few things I can complain about because she's funny and thoughtful and beautiful, so I tend to take advantage of the opportunities. She also puts up with a lot of terrible things about me including, but not limited to: farting, burping, and a really finicky penis (sometimes all three at the same time, depending on how liquored up I am). If she ever decides to write her own book, I'm screwed.

Yes. I had each guest go downstairs and put on ponchos and goggles. Some people were hesitant, given my "kill your own steak" party of 2011. But when they saw the paint and paintbrushes, they relaxed.

In the end, Kerri had a birthday gift that 40 of her closest friends had created *just for her*, and a gift that I was positive no other person in the world would have. You can see hearts and butterflies and swirls and handprints and splatters.

Even though *I* didn't make this for her, she called it one of the most thoughtful gifts she'd ever received. All the guests had a blast making it, and we had something else to adorn our walls.

Also remember, having her friends make this for her gave me those all-important and highly coveted "friend jealousy points," which go a long way toward that threesome we mentioned very early in the book.

I'll keep you posted if that ever works out.

Act 7 Progress Checklist

Now you have a whole bunch of ideas on how to keep romance in your relationship, even with kids around. Or you could always lock them in the basement.

	Yes	No
More head is always better.	☐	☒
Kids need to see that you're affectionate with your partner.	✓	☐
Picture collages are great romantic gifts, but only if you include close-ups of skulls.	☐	☒
Throwing paint is frigging awesome.	✓	☐
Always order the Romance Package when traveling with children.	☐	☒
French ticklers are actually from Belgium.	✓	☐
You shouldn't hide tiny penis drawings in paintings.	☐	☒
It's hard coming up with items for these checklists.	✓	☐

ACT 8 - MAINTENANCE MODE

Lather, Rinse, Repeat

The curtains rise and we see a living room set. There is a large television, coffee table, and couch. (If this was my house, there would be a chair with a slip cover falling off of it because none of the children know how to sit in my house if it doesn't involve leaping onto the furniture from three feet away at full speed. Drives me nuts.)

Beside the couch there is a bouquet of roses perched on a side table, and you can barely read the card: "To my favorite MILF."

Good job, buddy. Good job.

A man and a woman enter the living room and sit down next to each other. She sidles up next to him, rests her head on his shoulder, and puts her hand on his manly chest. He reaches down, seductively, and grabs the remote before she can think about.

He gives her a kiss on the forehead. She smiles.

"Porn?" he asks, aiming the remote at the television.

(Damn. Sorry. I keep forgetting this isn't my house.)

"Whatever you want," she replies. "I'm just comfy."

The man smiles and raises his legs to put his feet up on the coffee table. Before he rests them, he uses the heel of his foot to move a hardcover book out of the way. The cover reads, "Just Us," and has an oversized picture of the both of them, taken when they sat in a photo booth together while on vacation.

"I'm comfy too," he replies, and he turns the TV to "Busty Maids of Hoboken."

(Hey. Maybe this *is* my house.)

I. The Letter People

"Why don't you take a picture, it'll last longer." — **Pee Wee Herman**

When I was a kid, my family would go on vacations to Florida and California, and for some reason, Gettysburg, Pennsylvania. I can tell you that, as the son of someone who loved history and the story of the Civil War, there is no place worse to take your kids on a family vacation than to the sites of massacres and battles where thousands waged war.

Of course, I'm talking about Disneyland. After you've stood in line for three hours just to sit in a boat that breaks down in the middle of the "It's a Small World" ride where you have to listen to that godforsaken song for an hour straight, Gettysburg is a welcome respite.

My parents always made it a point to go on vacations each year so I could one day look back and say, "I don't remember that at ALL." In hindsight, I should have eaten more fish as a child because I don't remember anything, really. To this point, I just realized I went shopping this morning without wearing pants.

Luckily, I have a ton of photo albums to remind me about all the vacations my parents say we went on. Those pictures also remind me that I was an obese child who wore inappropriately short shorts and *OHMYGOD IS THAT MY TESTICLE HANGING OUT?*

It was with that visual in mind that I came up with the idea of making my own photo memories as gifts. It's always nice to revisit history with someone, unless it was spent stuck in a boat ride at Disneyland. Then you may want to destroy the evidence, like, immediately.

My God, I still have nightmares.

Sometimes when I'm thinking about doing something special for a gift I take a look back at all of the things I've done successfully before. And then I wish I had one of those devices they have in *Men in Black* where I can wipe out Kerri's memory and give her the same things over and over again.

Coming up with this crap is hard, yo. I didn't have a book like this for inspiration when I was trying to think of sweet things to do. I had to use my imagination, and you have absolutely NO IDEA how scary that can be if you're me. There are angry leprechaun centaurs throwing flaming cabbages and running amok in there.

I'll bet you're getting some idea now, though. Congrats.

There are only so many projects you can do with pictures of past events to turn them into unique and special gifts. By "only so many," I mean "two."

If you come up with a third one, please let me know because I'll add it to the "Special Edition" of this book in an attempt to rake in more money.

My kids need to go to college. Please spread the word. Thank you.

Kerri and I visited Faneuil Hall in Boston one afternoon (if you've never been to Faneuil Hall, I highly recommend it). It's an extremely large and historic marketplace full of street performers and artists and even a guy dressed like Benjamin Franklin. In fact, it was rated as the "Top Tourist Attraction that has a Guy Dressed like Benjamin Franklin" four out of the last five years.[1]

We stumbled upon a kiosk ("kiosk" is a Polish word meaning "Cart that sells key chains and sausages") that was selling a large number of black and white pictures. The pictures were random places and items, but each shared a common theme: They were photographed to resemble a letter of the alphabet.

A photo of the Eiffel Tower, for instance, looked like the letter "A," and the stanchion of the Brooklyn Bridge appeared to be an "H."

---

[1] The one year they lost was when the guy who dresses like Ben Franklin went to Scotland to visit family. That year, Loch Ness took the coveted "Top Tourist Attraction that has a Sea Monster" and "Top Tourist Location with a Guy Dressed like Ben Franklin" awards in a stunning double-whammy that shocked the world.

AH, I thought to myself.

I'll give you a moment with that one.

Above the photos were frames, each with several different photo cutouts in which the pictures were arranged to spell words.

- "Mommy"
- "Erin"
- "Yankees Suck"
- "F*ck Jeter"

Remember: This is Boston.

A genius and unique gift idea, I thought, until I realized that each frame was $50 or higher and each individual photo was $5, so writing "Nippletastic" would have cost me roughly $100—a hefty price to pay even though I think my dad would have gotten a kick out of it.

I decided this would be a great gift idea where I could make myself shine. It would be above and beyond the other way I make myself shine (by shaving my body extremely close and covering myself in baby oil). It really is quite a spectacle.

A tiny, shimmering spectacle.

My first step was to figure out what I wanted the picture to say, so I jotted down some good and some bad ideas:

Good Ideas

- Her name (this may not work for your situation if her name is "Mephistopheles" because this is going to cost you a small fortune for the frame alone)
- "Love"
- "Mine"
- "4Ever"

Bad Ideas

- Nippletastic
- This Photo:

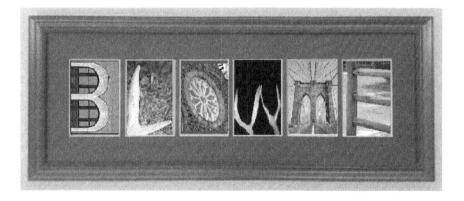

I decided to make the picture for my wife using the word "Love" because I'm cliché, but "Cliché" would have cost me more money for the frame. I'm also cheap. I'm not sure if you got that or not.

So with the word "Love" in mind, I set out to find items I could use to make the letters with. I wandered about the house looking for something resembling the letter "L." Several objects immediately jumped out at me:

- Corner of the stove.
- Two tampons juxtaposed in a drawer.
- My stepson making an "L" with his fingers on his forehead every time

I walked past him because he's mean to me.

Obviously none of these would fit the "romance" theme of the project, but then I happened to meander into my bedroom, and lo and behold, there was the hideous "frame of heads" I'd created from the previous craft (which had been rightly deemed too terrifying to display anyplace else in the house).

Quaking with fear, I approached the frame and focused in on the bottom left of the picture.

click

The perfect "L."

What made this even better was that the letter also included our pictures without the absolute horror of the remaining million tiny floating decapitations. I can't believe I screwed the pooch so badly on that gift. So not like me.

One letter down, three to go.

The letter "O" was pretty easy. I posed my wedding ring on a clean surface (which may be more difficult than you think if you live in a house with four children, as we do), and snapped a photo.

Voila.

The clean surface I used was the bedroom nightstand belonging to my neighbor's wife. She keeps a much cleaner house than ours. That's my reasoning, and I'm sticking with it.

I was exhausted at this point, and decided to call Kerri a new pet name for the next month: "Lo." I'd buy a frame with two photo cutouts and give her the "Lo" picture so I could stop worrying about finding two more letters.

Me: Hey, Lo.

Kerri: The hell?

Me: I'm going to call you "Lo" from now on because I like you on the down, Lo.

Kerri: No you won't call me that at all.

With my mind now made up for me, I went all out to find a "V" and "E" to finish the word. The "V" was taken from the "Harley Davidson" graphic on my motorcycle because she loves riding with me, and finding something else in the shape of a "V" was turning out to be impossible.

The only other "V" was on a tube of vaginal cream, and I didn't want to be

reminded about feminine itch and odor every time I looked at this thing on my wall.

So, Harley Davidson "V" it was.

The "E" took some fancy finagling, but let's see if you can guess what it is.

To help you guess, I should have included pictures of the bite marks I got while attempting this. That is my dog's tail and hind feet, forming an "E" shape as he was lying down. I had to maneuver him around a little bit to get it just right, which he apparently hated very much. If you plan on doing this, and your dog is more vicious than mine, I highly suggest finding something else to make an "E" out of. I do not recommend you use a cat (see earlier chapter).

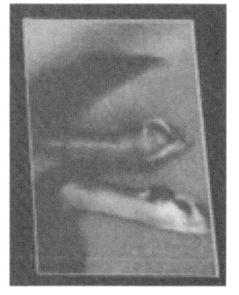

With all the photos taken, it was just a matter of arranging them inside the frame. I arranged the letters facing the glass and then turned it over.

"VOLE"

Ah, shit.

I pulled the thing apart and reordered them. I guess what I'm saying is, "Pay close attention to the order in which you assemble the photos, because a woman receiving a gift that insinuates she's a small rodent may yield undesired results."

And here's my finished product:

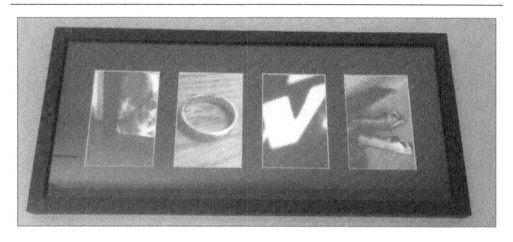

Cool, right?

BONUS IDEA

This is also another one of those projects you can use as gifts for Christmas, birthdays, Mother's Day, etc. and can give to pretty much anyone. If you have kids, try using the children to pose for the letters to make signs that say "Grandma" or "Grammy" or "Mommy" or "Daddy" or "Guy who comes over to visit mommy every Saturday."

I have scars from my childhood.

Using the kids as the letters is a great way to include them in gifts for your relatives. However, I can tell you that getting a 4-year-old to hold a backbend so you can make a letter "G" is an exercise in patience, several emergency room visits, and a possible spinal surgery.

You've been warned.

Other than that, have fun with the project. They'll vole it.

Love it, I mean. They'll love it.

See? I told you the letter ordering is important.

II. Giving Her the TP Treatment

DATE NIGHT.

Every couple needs one.

By the end of the work week, you're both junk. Your wife has just spent 60 hours on her feet working in a dental office, and you've just spent 40 hours trapped in a cubicle, Tweeting and updating Facebook 90% of the time. The other 10% was spent revising final edits for a book, perhaps. Or maybe working.

whistles

So one Saturday I decided to treat my wife to the old standby of date nights: *dinner and a show.*

When you both work and still have to take care of four kids, "dinner and a show" means "chicken nuggets and screaming at the kitchen table." You're probably thinking, *How is screaming at the kitchen table considered a "show,"* but that's because you've never seen my wife scream. It's really quite spectacular.

Unbeknownst to her, I booked a sitter and scored us tickets to *Blue Man Group*. She had never seen the show before, and I thought she'd like it since they vomit Twinkies halfway through.

Who doesn't like seeing people vomiting up sponge cake? RIGHT. That's exactly what I thought, too, so I got us front row tickets, because if you're going to experience *Blue Man Group,* you should get some Twinkie on you. I need to work for their marketing department.

She was excited and surprised, of course. Spontaneity always helps with relationship maintenance, unless you're spontaneously combusting. Then you just burn the other person and some good furniture, so don't do that.

The first indication that something was amiss was when we were handed ponchos as we entered the theater.

Kerri: What are these for?

Me: We're in the poncho section!

Kerri was not enthused, which was weird, because usually she got excited when I put on a poncho. In her defense, though, I look pretty awesome wearing nothing but a poncho and goggles.

Our sex nights are crazy.

She glanced at me sideways as we headed to our seats. I helped slip her poncho on, and she helped me with mine. We sat back and craned our necks up to the stage.

Me: FRONT ROW.

Kerri: Ponchos. I'm scared.

Me: It's going to be awesome—*adjusts poncho*—Is it, like, really hot in here?

We were front row, center-stage, with spotlights and all kinds of laser things bearing down upon us. The ponchos had begun to act like oven roasting bags, and I'm pretty sure if I had some carrots and onions I could have made a nice dinner out of myself. Sweat rolled down my face, and I glanced at my wife, miserably sweating inside her own plastic cocoon.

Me: FRONT ROW.

She did not acknowledge me. It wasn't a good sign.

Thankfully, the show began and the mood changed. Yes, we'd each lost 15 pounds in the first half-hour of the show, but we were having fun. She was laughing, and I was laughing, and I was sweating, and OHMYGOD I AM LAVA, but yes, we were having an amazing time.

That is, until, the finale.

The end of the *Blue Man Show* involves toilet paper and audience participation. The last time I experienced a finale with toilet paper and audience participation was in that hotel room in Vegas, so I was not looking forward to waking up in a shower again, covered in poo.

And why the Blue Men have a TP finale I do not know. Somewhere, I'm sure, is a thesis about the significance of toilet paper as it relates to the conclusion of a *Blue Man Show*. In all honesty, that's a pretty crappy thesis.

As the finale began, miles upon miles of toilet paper suddenly uncoiled from the balcony and rained down upon everyone on the floor. As the toilet paper barrage began to smother those at the rear of the auditorium, ushers told them to push it forward toward the stage.

Push it forward.

Toward the stage.

The stage we were sitting in front of.

We've all seen footage of deadly avalanches cascading down upon skiers, hikers, slow squirrels, and entire villages. Now imagine an overwhelming and dangerous avalanche is approaching you, but the wall of snow is actually a 4-foot high, 80-foot wide pile of Charmin.

I looked at my wife.

She looked at me.

And that's when ...

The wall of toilet paper crashed upon us. I tried to hurl the paper onto the stage, but I'm tiny and have little arms. I tried to push back against the avalanche, but it was no use. The excess weight indicated it was heavily fortified paper, the kind typically used in Mexican restaurant bathrooms.

I fought my way around to find Kerri.

SHE WAS GONE.

There was no sign of her. I clawed paper out of the way, hoisting it to the stage in a frantic effort to find her, but it was no use. She had been washed away to a better place. I had no choice but to soldier on and find another woma—

Muffled Voice: I'm ... getting ... sick ...

SHE'S ALIVE!

Me: I'M COMING FOR YOU, HONEY!

I tried. I really made a valiant effort, but the sheer volume of toilet paper coming at us versus what I could actually move made it a losing battle. Eventually, I succumbed to the idea of having to bury her and move on. Every so often, though, I could hear signs of life:

Kerri: ... throw up ...

Kerri: ... Rodney is sexy ...

Kerri: ... help ...

Kerri: ... Twinkie ...

After what seemed like an eternity, the Charmin deluge subsided. I dredged my wife out of the bottomless abyss of bathroom tissue. She emerged disheveled and exhausted.

On the bright side, the paper did an amazing job of cleaning the Twinkie residue off of our ponchos.

The rest of the audience gave a standing ovation. That seemed to make sense at the time because aside from nearly suffocating it was a good show. We fought the urge to pass out and clapped along with the rest of the audience who, just moments before, had tried to murder us.

Kerri's hair was matted, and her mascara had run. Except for the exhausted smile, I would have thought she was the undead. The poncho was stuck to her like melted Saran Wrap. I peeled it off.

Me: You're a little sweaty.

Kerri: FRONT ROW.

Point taken. Next time we do this on date night, we'll try the balcony.

III. Say "Cheesy"

Kerri: I hope nothing ever happens to this computer.

Me: I know. We've spent a lot on this porn collection.

Kerri: No. Well, that, plus we'll lose all our pictures.

light bulb

A few years had passed, and Kerri and I had amassed a lot of photos of each other. Most of these photos had to be deleted due to storage limitations on our phones and the fact our kids kept guessing our lock passcodes.

Because of this, sext pics are usually the first things to get deleted.

The rest of the pictures were posted into albums on the computer. This practice, though, tends to get messy when you're looking for a particular photo and—whoop—there you are full-frontal from 1992 wearing a Mr. T Mohawk.

I think I pulled off the look quite well.

Kerri had a point. I didn't want my laptop to crash, or have my social media accounts locked—seriously, it was ONE TIME, Mr. President—or my cloud hacked, or my cloud account crash-locked and cyber-bullied (I'm sorry to throw all those terms at you, but I'm a techie).

I had to save our photos. Maybe in some kind of picture book?

But it would be a lot different than the last "picture book" I gave her, which was a small notebook, and if you flipped the pages you could see two stick figures having sex.

I have a lot of free time.

I downloaded most of the pictures we had (minus the ones of things that resemble penises) from a Facebook album titled, "Things that look like penises." My timeline has been flagged for inappropriateness so many times I have a plaque at Facebook headquarters.

I wanted to make a graphic novel of our relationship while also creating something that she could use as kindling if we ever broke up. Always give her a backup plan, guys. Seriously, this book is chock-full of things that will allow her to hold her own Burning Man event if you guys ever split.

I organized pictures from our earliest memories as a couple to photos taken the previous weekend, and uploaded them to a site that made the book for me. All I had to do was add captions. You'd think that would be easy, but I use so many swear words that half the pages were Autocorrected to things like:

"This is where we fudged the shot out of each otter."

Honestly, that sounds hysterical. I should have left it that way.

The result was a hardcover book that was so stunning and professional that it's sitting on my coffee table as I write this. Of course, that's because I placed it there so I could take a picture of it:

It's titled, *"Just Us – Rodney and Kerri in pictures."*

PRO TIP: If you're keeping this on the coffee table, make sure you have pants on in the pictures. You never know who the hell is gonna open that damn thing one day, and **BOOM**, you lose custody of the children.

And another reason to avoid adding pictures of your Mr. Wiggly is that pop-up books cost extra.

Needless to say, Kerri loved the book. This may be partly because I snuck "I will love all things Rodney gives me" into her wedding vows.

The picture on the right is absolutely one of my favorite in the world, and it's just this stupid thing where I pretended to feed tiny Kerri to a triceratops. Your *dinosaur-feeding-photos* may vary, but if you have one like this, I highly recommend adding it to the book.

I've learned (during some arguments) that the hard corners are extra deadly. So if she holds the book like a ninja throwing star, she can make me run really, really fast in the opposite direction. This paragraph is begging for another disclaimer.

If you decide to make a picture book (and you definitely should), you've just shown her you cherish your memories together, and they're literally sitting on your coffee table for others to enjoy.

Unless you're not wearing pants. I can't stress enough how much you should put the book in a drawer somewhere if you're not wearing pants. For the kids' sake.

IV. Is It Hump Day?

Her: Do you know what today is?

If you just had a heart attack reading that sentence, there's a damn good chance you're a guy. If you're not a guy and had a heart attack reading that, you may be a woman with a very bad memory. If you had a heart attack for any other reason, you should see your Cardiologist.

Her: Do you know what today is?

GAH.

Quickly, your mind scatters into a million synaptic impulses, like a hoard of cockroaches when someone turns on the light. Each little insect has his own unique job trying to hunt down the answer and report back to the center of your brain so you can formulate a response.

Cockroach #1: Today is October 17th, sir!

You: Thank you, minion. That doesn't ring a bell. Shit.

Cockroach #2: Her birthday is in June.

You: Okay. That's not it. June? Really? June what?

Cockroach #2: I just got June, sir.

You: Shit. Okay. Remind me to look that up later.

Cockroach #3: Your anniversary is November 23, sir!

You: Ah, yes. I remember because it was two days before Thanksgiving turkey. I like turkey.

You glance around at your memory minions, all frantically searching for the answer. No holidays match. No anniversaries. There are no surgeries scheduled.

One cockroach is sitting in the corner drumming his finger over his lips and making that "brrbbrbbbrbbrrbb" sound.

Cockroach #4: Sir, the closest we can find is your dad's birthday four days ago.

You: Maybe that's it. Maybe she messed it up.

Much like the "WHY do you love me?" horrible question from earlier, this particular query has doomed many a man. That's because, after not answering her for 30 seconds, she follows with this one:

Her: You DO know what today is, right?

You glance over at your "memory cockroaches." They shrug their little cockroach shoulders.

You: My dad's ... birth ... day ... ?

Her jaw drops and her eyes harden. She throws an envelope into your lap that says "Babe" with little hearts drawn on it.

Her: It's the anniversary of when we met. Five years ago today. And your father's birthday was Thursday, jerk.

Oh.

Well. Okay. Now you don't feel so bad you got it wrong, because this was a needle-in-a-haystack question.

You: And how the hell was I supposed to know that?

Her eyes widen and smoke curls from her ears.

This will not end well for me, you think.

Her: I know it because it's the day my life changed forever. You should know it, too, for the same reason.

And that, my friends, is why women are batshit crazy. Women remember every single detail of every single moment in your miserable history together. There are very few exceptions to this rule, but for the most part, a woman's mind is a steel trap when it comes to specific memories and dates.

They do not even need to be important. If a woman knows the particular date that something happened on, she can also tell you—down to the very last fiber—what she wore and when she bought it. How a woman can remember minutiae such as this—but can't keep up with the plot of the *Bourne Identity* and has to keep pausing it to ask you what the crap is going on—is a mystery for the ages.

I, personally, have the memory of a potato and have to keep looking back to the last paragraph to see if I've already written this same sentence. I've been burned by the *what-day-it-is* question so many times I can't keep count, mainly because I have the memory of a potato.

rim shot

This very *what-day-it-is* scenario I've described happened to me one fine October 17th. I had zero idea it was the anniversary of the day we met, because honestly, I didn't care. I didn't think it was something anyone kept track of.

All I knew was that I was glad we met. The exact day was irrelevant.

But it wasn't irrelevant to her.

There's a saying that goes, "If it's important to you, it's important to me." This is usually one-sided because football and hockey are important to me, and no female ever cares about them.

On the flip side, wardrobe choices are important to women, but most guys don't give a crap what they put on as long as we can get out of the house on time for once.

I guess what I'm saying is, "Not all sayings are applicable for all situations."

Since this date we met was important to her, I decided to treat it as such. I ran through her entire Facebook timeline to find out when she changed her statuses and to what. I also dug around to see if she made any notes about milestones, and sure enough, there was an "our first kiss" status.

I should honestly talk to her about her need to overshare.

EDITOR'S NOTE: Bwahahahahahaha! Pot, meet Kettle.

So to stay out of hot water and get back on her good side, I had this made:

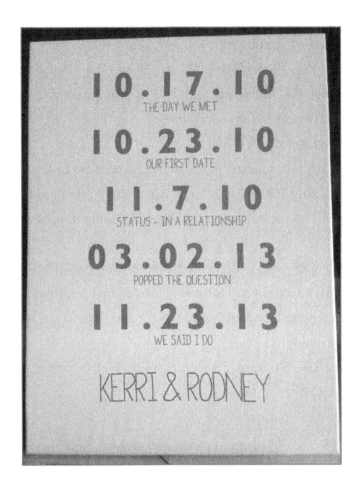

The best thing about this gift is that it's also a gift FOR ME. Now, I will never forget a date or be sucker-punched by that stupid question ever again. All I have to do is glance over to the wall, and voila, I have the answer.

I might even fire my memory cockroaches. Fire them, that is, once they get me the definitive date of her birthday. I forgot to put that on the poster.

V. Rubbing Off On the Wife

Yeah, I wish it was that kind of book.

After four years of putting up with my homemade gifts and crafts and projects and presents, my wife decided to get into the spirit of it on our First Anniversary. I was 46, half-blind, and deaf by this point, and kept forgetting who she was, but her effort was admirable.

I am not aging gracefully AT ALL.

I'm not saying my wife doesn't give good gifts because I like having sex and don't feel like getting into an argument when she reads this. I'm just saying that—and she will be the first to admit this—it's something she's never really tried to do.

So, on our first anniversary, I received a large, wrapped gift. I was expecting the usual presents of beef jerky or candy or candied beef jerky. What I got, though, was something completely and utterly amazing:

Beef jerky *and* candy.

WAIT. It wasn't JUST beef jerky and candy. No! It was a basket of beef jerky and candy with a note typed, printed, cut out with fancy scissors, pasted to construction paper and thoughtfully taped to EACH ITEM. The outside of the basket also had a message taped to it like so:

What is this sorcery? I thought. *Who are you and what have you done with my wife?*

Every note was a sweet, hand-made message just for me. I was floored.

The beef jerky (you thought I was joking) and gummy bears:

The Junior Mints and Reese's Pieces:

Even the Mixed Nuts and Symphony Bar:

And then, to top it all off, the Almond Joy (so gross, by the way):

That gift? It was amazing. I was shocked. I was hungry. I was hungry and shocked. But mostly I was speechless. And for anyone who knows me, I'm never speechless.

Then, expecting the gift-giving to return to normal, on Valentine's Day 2015, Kerri raised the bar. Below my usual presents of chocolate-covered raisins and more gummy bears[1] was a small wrapped gift (right).

"I Love You Because ... A Keepsake Journal of Our Love"

So cute. She totally stole my book idea and turned the tables on me. How origin—

But then I opened the book. This was an actual notebook. Inside were her own notes, handwritten, over the next 50 pages or so. Each page had three or

---

[1] I'm pretty sure my wife is trying to kill me via saturated fats disguised as trinkets.

more prompts followed by blank lines to write answers on, like:

> ***You make me feel ...***

What I thought she'd write: "*You make me feel ...* your testicles when I'm fast asleep."

What she actually wrote: "*You make me feel ...* loved."

> ***I love when you ...***

What I thought she'd write: "*I love when you ...* think I'm asleep and try to make me feel your testicles."

What she actually wrote: "*I love when you ...* tell me you love me."

Dammit. I'm horrible at this game.

The notes went on and on. Page after page I read, in her own words and handwriting, about how she felt and things she loved about us. She mangled the spelling of "cunnilingus," but I figured I'd let it slide because the gift was so awesome.

That is, until I got here (actual page from my book). Great.

She told me she didn't leave this blank on purpose, but the coincidence of it being this particular page that she skipped seems suspect.

Even with this page blank, it was pretty awesome to read about all the reasons why she's nuts about me. I'm nuts about her, too, but I'm still not eating that Almond Joy.

So gross.

Act 8 Progress Checklist

Companies make their money from MAINTENANCE CONTRACTS. I made that up, but companies that sell these contracts have massive profit margins. This is why most products suck, since the company makes more money selling you services to help fix stuff you bought from them.

In relationship terms, maintenance can be one of the most important contributions and have the greatest return on investment. If you want things to keep working smoothly, you have to regularly work on the upkeep.

Holy shit. That actually sounded insightful. Let's see what you've learned.

	Yes	No
I really like beef jerky.	✓	☐
Feminine hygiene boxes are great for some romantic project ideas.	☐	✗
You could go for some beef jerky, now that you're thinking about it.	✓	☐
There are a billion things you can do with your photos.	✓	☐
Did you buy beef jerky yet?	☐	✗
Milestone relationship dates are important to most women.	✓	☐
If you do go get jerky, can you get me some, too? Thank you.	✓	☐

THE STUNNING CONCLUSION

The actors line up on the stage and face the wildly clapping audience. Arm in arm, they take a group bow:

"BRAVO!"

"Encore!"

"There's a white Honda Civic in the parking lot with its lights on!"

"Oh shit, my Viagra kicked in early. I think I'll stay seated."

They exit stage right, and one by one, the major players return to center stage to accept their own applause. Chivalry, Love Note, Picture Book,

Horrifying Floating-Head Collage, Romantic Bag of Beef Jerky, Just-Because Card, and the Love-Explosion Painting greet the crowd. The people, now in a standing ovation, begin to throw roses that immediately stain the stage and the wardrobes of the players, and everyone begins to get pissed off.

curtain closes

I had no real title for this section, so I chose "The Stunning Conclusion." Please note there is nothing stunning about this conclusion other than a sincere lack of being stunning, which is stunning in itself.

I did accidentally write "The Stunning Concussion" because Autocorrect really sucks, and this is why my editor gets the fee he does. Right now you'd be wondering why I'd have a concussion unless one of the gifts I wrote about didn't go over very well. Obviously this would never happen because HAVE YOU READ THIS BOOK?

Exactly.

I hope I was able to give you some new and innovative ideas on how to make your relationship—no matter what stage it's in—a little more squishy in the heart parts. I can tell you from experience that squishy hearts lead to harder *other things* on the regular, so if that's what you're aiming for, I'd get started on some of these projects. Stat.

At the very least, you'll get the well-deserved attention and adoration of others. If you're a guy, you'll also garner the hatred of any other man who got wind of the amazingly romantic things you've done, because they'll look terrible in their own relationship.

For this latter scenario, I suggest you sign up for karate at the nearest dojo. Maybe you and your lover can take it together as a couple—there you go, one more romantic suggestion on the way out the door.

"Love Nunchucks," we'll call that one, and who knows, maybe you'll need that martial arts training to keep all your woman's friends at bay after they fall for you, too. Or maybe just invite them in, right? The more the merrier, eh?

Eyes on the prize, boys.

Eyes on the prize.

Acknowledgments

A lot of people helped me out with the creation of this book and its heavy editing. Trust me when I say this thing was *way worse*, originally. I can't write for shit. In addition, a lot of people assisted me in reviewing and critiquing *all* of my works, and for the most part, have gone unmentioned except for blanket words of appreciation. I'm here to right those wrongs, and if I've forgotten you in some way, please know it was most likely intentional. Just kidding. Maybe.

Thanks to (in order of sexiness and/or the way they popped into my head):

My wife, my kids, my wife's kids, my friends/fans/followers, my mom, Tim Caviness, Noreen Conway for all the cool illustrations throughout the book, Christina Evans for designing the book's cover, Suzy Soro, Kris Wehrmeister, Linda Doty, Julie Zantopoulos, Elizabeth Catalano, Sarah del Rio, the amazing women of the Sin City Bounty Radio Show (particularly Sue McCann), Monique Cocco, James Mulligan, Fox 25 Morning News in Boston (waves at Gene Lavanchy), anyone who has ever hosted me on a blog/book tour, Ginger Ann (the Tuesday daytime stripper at the Golden Banana for her, um, support), all of the amazing and talented people who have appeared on my book covers and provided their editorial reviews for all the world to see.

For those last people, I know how difficult it must have been to endorse something as ridiculous as the crap I write, and for that courage, I thank you. If you're reading this, please make sure you check out all of my editorial cover reviews and then go follow or friend those people because they are all amazing. I'm not just saying that to get out of paternity suits, either, in most of the cases.

Most of all I'd like to thank you for buying this book and helping me get one step closer to quitting my job and writing this drivel full-time. I am truly grateful.

About the Author

Rodney Lacroix lives in southern New Hampshire. He is the proud biological father of two amazing children and step-ological father of two step-amazing stepchildren. He also likes to invent terms. Rodney is married to a gorgeous woman way out of his league, and—even with that—is still trying to score boob pics from his female Twitter followers. He's a guy, after all. He has an awesome rescue dog named Jax who appeared on the family Christmas card, portraying every member in the Nativity Scene. Rodney also has too much time on his hands to do stuff like that, but seriously, it was hysterical.

Rodney is a black-belt in Kenpo Karate, has won multiple tournament awards, and was given the title of Sensei at his dojo in 2014. Rodney is terrified of spiders because they're scary and are not impressed at all that he knows karate. He also likes to put random facts about himself in the "About the Author" sections of his books.

Rodney's previous two books, *Things Go Wrong for Me* and *Perhaps I've Said Too Much* have won him multiple humor awards and have appeared on international best-seller lists. He's hoping this book gets him the trifecta, and by the time you read this, he hopes it's allowed him to retire to a life of luxury where he can afford *Dragon, Naturally Speaking* so he doesn't have to type any more. Typing tires him out. Also, Rodney is lazy.

FOR LADIES ONLY

Psst. You.

Yes, you.

opens trench coat

Sorry, sorry. That's just a force of habit when I have a woman's attention. Let's start over.

Dear Ladies,

I know there's a good chance that many of you reading this are women. I happen to have a large female following which is a direct result of how I look in a bathrobe. I can't blame you, really.

The women who have purchased this book fall into one of four categories:

- Those looking for a humorous male perspective on romantic tips.
- The ones looking for new ideas on romance for themselves and are sick of doing the same old bullshit.
- My mom (thanks, mom).
- Women who have bought this book in the hopes their man will read it.

It's that last point I want to address, because if that is your intent, it's a little weird that I'm complicit in helping you manipulate your man. I don't want to manipulate your man. I did a short overnight stint in protective custody once, and that's as much man-manipulation that I ever want to do.

But, hey, let's do this. Here are some ideas on how to slip this book to him without getting him mad:

- Tell him if he liked that thing you did after reading *Fifty Shades of Grey*, then if he reads this, he'll get Round 2 of that craziness.
- Write *"There's a (insert sexual favor that you're not ashamed to do here) at the end of this book"* on the inside cover.
- Leave it as the only reading material in the bathroom.

Be sure to rip this page out and don't mention my name, OK? I don't want to be tossed out of Mantown for breaking the Bro Code.

One more thing ... good luck.

CPSIA information can be obtained at www.ICGtesting.com
Printed in the USA
BVOW10s1935220815

414597BV00008B/24/P